Rape Culture and Spiritual Violence

Rape Culture and Spiritual Violence examines sexual violence against women, how religion and society contribute to a rape culture, and the extreme suffering endured by rape victims as a result. Using the testimony of women who have experienced both rape and the consequences of rape culture – from a range of religious, cultural, ethnic, and social contexts – the book explores both the suffering and healing of rape victims from World War II to today.

Among the issues considered are victim invisibility, the inability to express pain, and the tendency to assume shame and self-blame. The study examines the role of society in shaping and reinforcing these responses, contributing to traumas that can lead to spiritual death. The book also explores possibilities for multiple spiritual resurrections within the practice of daily life, encouraging both individual healing and social change.

Gina Messina-Dysert is Dean of the School of Graduate and Professional Studies at Ursuline College, USA, and co-founder and co-director of the Feminism and Religion project (http://feminismandreligion.com).

Religion and Violence
Edited by Lisa Isherwood, *University of Winchester, UK* and
Rosemary Radford Ruether, *Claremont Graduate University, USA*

1. **Reweaving the Relational Mat**
   A Christian Response to Violence Against Women from Oceania
   Joan Filemoni-Tofaeono and Lydia Johnson

2. **America, Amerikkka**
   Elect Nation and Imperial Violence
   Rosemary Radford Ruether

3. **Weep Not for Your Children**
   Essays on Religion and Violence
   Lisa Isherwood and Rosemary Radford Ruether

4. **In Search of Solutions**
   The Problem of Religion and Conflict
   Clinton Bennett

5. **Shalom/Salaam/Peace**
   A Liberation Theology of Hope
   Constance A. Hammond

6. **Faith-Based War**
   From 9/11 to Catastrophic Success in Iraq
   T. Walter Herbert

7. **The Real Peace Process**
   Worship, Politics and the End of Sectarianism
   Siobhan Garrigan

8. **A Cry for Dignity**
   Religion, Violence and the Struggle of Dalit Women in India
   Mary Grey

9 **U.S. War-Culture, Sacrifice and Salvation**
   Kelly Denton-Borhaug

10 **Edith Stein and Regina Jonas**
   Religious Visionaries in the Time of the Death Camps
   Emily Leah Silverman

11 **Rape Culture and Spiritual Violence**
   Religion, Testimony, and Visions of Healing
   Gina Messina-Dysert

Rape Culture and Spiritual Violence
Religion, Testimony, and Visions of Healing

Gina Messina-Dysert

LONDON AND NEW YORK

First published 2015
by Routledge
2 Park Square, Milton Park, Abingdon, Oxon OX14 4RN

and by Routledge
711 Third Avenue, New York, NY 10017

Routledge is an imprint of the Taylor & Francis Group, an informa business

© 2015 Gina Messina-Dysert

The right of Gina Messina-Dysert to be identified as author of this work has been asserted by her in accordance with sections 77 and 78 of the Copyright, Designs and Patents Act 1988.

All rights reserved. No part of this book may be reprinted or reproduced or utilized in any form or by any electronic, mechanical, or other means, now known or hereafter invented, including photocopying and recording, or in any information storage or retrieval system, without permission in writing from the publishers.

Trademark notice: Product or corporate names may be trademarks or registered trademarks, and are used only for identification and explanation without intent to infringe.

British Library Cataloguing-in-Publication Data
A catalogue record for this book is available from the British Library

Library of Congress Cataloging-in-Publication Data
A catalog record for this title has been requested

ISBN: 978-1-844-65788-9 (hbk)
ISBN: 978-1-315-74460-5 (ebk)

Typeset in Times New Roman
by Taylor and Francis Books

For my mother, Maria.

Contents

Preface	x
Acknowledgements	xii
1 Introduction	1
2 Rape culture ordained by God?	5
3 Learning from women's testimony	26
4 A preliminary analysis of sexual violence and rape culture	61
5 Sexual violence, *han*, and spiritual death	83
6 Spiritual resurrection: *Han-Pu-Ri* and momentary salvation	100
7 Conclusion	111
Bibliography	116
Index	125

Preface

This project has long been on my mind. I began my advocacy and activism focused on ending violence against women at the young age of eighteen; although more than two decades have passed, sadly little has changed. There are still high rates of sexual assault and a culture that blames and shames the victim is alive and well; although we do see that the rape culture is evolving alongside society. As demonstrated by the rape case in Steubenville, Ohio – which has become known as "Steubenville" – with new technology our rape culture has become more complex, perpetrating abuse in new ways.[1]

Having worked directly in the field of rape and domestic violence, I have encountered countless women who experienced sexual assault. The wounding these women suffered ran deep. While physical wounds healed, spiritual wounds persisted, with many women speaking of feeling shame and blame for the abuse perpetrated against them. This said, I must also acknowledge that with statistics demonstrating that one in three women worldwide have experienced sexual assault, I have also witnessed the wounding so many women in my own life have suffered as a result of such brutality. However, it was not until I learned of my own mother's experience perpetrated by the rape culture that I realized the necessity of completing this project. Despite the fact that I had multiple years of experience working with victims of gender-based violence, I never realized my own mother could be counted among those statistics.

My mother's life was plagued with suffering, and although I could see that her spirit was wounded, I did not know why. After she passed away, I learned of the horrors she had experienced in her life. The assault left her despondent and the rape culture inflicted such shame that she never revealed her victimization.

Rape culture perpetrated a life of suffering against my mother and she died without having the opportunity to speak of her *han*.[2] However, through this project I am giving voice to the anguish she endured, to the injustice she experienced in her life. Through the voices of other women who have shared her experience of sexual violence, my mother's *han* will be spoken and heard, and, consequently, the culture of silence will be disrupted. It is only through the interruption of this culture of silence and confronting the injustices suffered by women as a result of rape culture that healing can begin. Thus, this project is embarked on in the spirit of *Han-Pu-Ri*.[3]

Notes

1 The Steubenville rape case will be further discussed in Chapter 4.
2 *Han* is a Korean concept that describes a compressed suffering of multiple feelings and pain. This concept will be discussed throughout this study.
3 *Han-Pu-Ri* is a shamanistic ritual primarily led by women that releases *han* and offers healing. This concept will be explored as a path for spiritual resurrection within this study.

Acknowledgements

A multitude of individuals have offered contributions in many forms to this work. While it would be impossible to acknowledge everyone formally, I would like to take this opportunity to demonstrate my gratitude for all who have engaged me in discussions about my research and offered encouragement along the way.

I am particularly grateful to Rosemary Radford Ruether, who has been an incredible mentor to me and has offered me guidance and support when it was needed most. In addition, I must express my appreciation for Claudia Bushman, Karen Jo Torjesen, Tammi J. Schneider, and Pamela Brubaker, who provided direction and nurturing along my journey.

To the community of women from Claremont Graduate University, Lisa Maldonado, Cynthia Garrity-Bond, Catherine Dundas-Reyas, Caroline Kline, Lachelle Schilling, Kate Sargent, and Juliana Denson, who helped me to recognize my own theological voice through countless hours of deep conversation and feminist exploration. Their constant encouragement allowed me to learn to trust myself and embrace my journey. Their feminist passion and spirit have continually inspired me.

To my friend, colleague, and mentor Joseph R. LaGuardia, whose skills, talent, and competencies have become my benefit.

To my family, especially my father, Biagio Messina, who has continually encouraged me and offered support. And to my beautiful and intelligent daughter Sarah, who at the young age of four already claims feminist status and questions why as a girl she is limited by society, excluded from particular roles such as priest, and why she is sometimes referred to as a "guy" when she is really a woman. I hope her future is one free of rape culture.

Finally, to my amazing husband and partner, Chris Messina-Dysert. I have only been able to complete this work because of his unwavering love and support; he truly is my pillar and it is impossible to adequately express my gratitude to him.

1 Introduction

"A fate worse than death" is a common phrase utilized to describe rape. In fact, for many victims[1] of rape, physical death is preferable. While, for some victims, the goal is survival regardless of the brutality they will endure, for others "once their body has been sexually violated, life is not worth living – the most sacred and private parts of their bodily integrity have been invaded and they will never feel whole or safe again."[2] This sentiment was expressed loudly during World War II on June 25, 1943, when twenty-four Jewish girls were raped by SS soldiers. After being brutally assaulted they were offered their lives if they agreed to become sex slaves for the German guards. The girls refused and chose death "either because they had already been sexually assaulted and could not live with this gross bodily invasion, or because they could not bear the reality that they might have to endure more sexual assault."[3]

Sexual violence targets the core of a woman's personhood and is an attack on her basic human rights. This form of violence transcends all boundaries, causing destructive consequences not only to the physical but also to the spiritual health of women. Because of the taboo nature of rape as well as the societal response induced by the assault, rape is especially harmful and results in the wounding of the woman's interiority, damaging her connection with her true self and leading to continuous suffering. "The way women feel about themselves and their environment is permanently altered by the incidence of intimate assault in their lives."[4]

Rape culture pervades society and is present in every culture where rape and other forms of sexual violence are common and widespread. In a rape culture victim blaming is commonplace and those who have been raped suffer some sort of community rejection and punishment. Women are seen as inferior and deserving of the violence perpetrated against them, causing an additional victimization or "second rape." This treatment of victims triggered by rape culture transpires in every society where rape occurs. Rape culture must be understood as a key component of the suffering endured by the rape victim; thus the destruction to a rape victim's spiritual health occurs despite cultural boundaries and is experienced regardless of ethnicity, religion, class, or other qualifying factors.[5]

The construction of *han*

The experience of sexual violence within a rape culture results in *han*, the compression of multiple sufferings that Andrew Sung Park describes as "a slow death of the spirit" resulting from "sadness, resignation, hopelessness, and despair."[6] Although *han* is a traditional Korean concept and term, it is fitting to apply it to both the collective suffering of rape victims and the individual suffering endured by women following a sexual assault because it is a term that properly articulates the overall experience of a compressed suffering that wounds the spirit and results in a spiritual death. As Beverly Lanzetta explains, "What harms a woman's soul reverberates in her physical, emotional, and mental spheres, generating suffering in every area of her life."[7]

This study will define spiritual death and explore how the experience of the violent act of rape within a rape culture constructs *han*. Furthermore, it will identify rape culture as being alarmingly widespread, manifested in multiple contexts across borders, and demonstrate that the occurrence of *han* and possibility of spiritual death is experienced by victims regardless of cultural, religious, or class dividers.[8] Specific attention will be given to the victims' inability to express pain as well as assumed qualities of shame, self-blame, and invisibility. Societal response and its ability to provoke these qualities, further contributing to the emotional and spiritual trauma which can ultimately result in a spiritual death, will be examined. Finally, the possibility for multiple spiritual resurrections through various practices, including the application of the traditional practice of *Han-Pu-Ri*, a Korean shamanistic ritual that releases *han*, will be explored.

Methodology

The analysis of this study will focus on the testimonies of women found in non-fiction literature who have experienced sexual violence. The testimonies presented will examine the occurrence of rape in different cultural and social settings during the time period framed by the World War II era and the present day. Each testimony will offer insight into suffering endured as a result of the rape itself followed by suffering instigated by community response to the victim as well as the totality of the consequences of such suffering. In addition, stories of women from the past will be lifted up in order to document the ongoing legacy of sexual violence.

Note that the accounts of sexual violence provided by the testimonies will be described carefully and in detail with several purposes. First, such description will provide testimony to the voices of the victims. In addition, by describing and naming the crime, this taboo will be confronted and the silence demanded of rape victims will be broken. Finally, providing the details of the crime acknowledges the shamefulness of the act by the perpetrator while affirming the victim and freeing her from misplaced guilt and shame. Other atrocious crimes and their victims are openly disclosed in minute detail whereas rape is shrouded in secrecy. Treating sexual violence as taboo displaces blame on to the victim, shifting it away from its rightful place – the perpetrator.

While some claim that providing details of sexual assault is comparable to pornography, I assert that this claim is representative of the many reasons that rape crimes have been historically ignored and their victims shamed and silenced. Furthermore, explicit details demand attention and impress images into the mind whereas generic descriptions are easily ignored and forgotten. The "pressure-cooker" theory[9] of male nature is dismissed and the violent act is recognized for what it is. By carefully describing these accounts of rape, continued conversation around sexual violence will be encouraged.

The examples offered will not be the most sinister or disturbing of the violence committed against women; rather, they are routine examples of rape which are committed around the globe in various cultures and social situations every day, every hour, and every minute.

Synopsis

The study will be broken down into seven chapters, including this introduction, and will give attention to the stories of women who have experienced sexual violence. Chapter 2 will examine rape within religion. Biblical "rape texts" and their interpretations that support rape culture will be reviewed. In addition, purity legends and virgin martyrdom will be explored. The chapter will discuss the pervasive manifestation of rape culture within these elements of religion as a means to control women's sexuality and encourage shame and blame of rape victims.

Chapter 3 discusses the importance of women's testimony and consists of twenty-five cases from non-fiction literary sources that offer the testimonies of women from past and present who have experienced rape in their lives. The cases present the stories of women from different cultural, racial, and religious backgrounds and are spread across multiple types of rape, including stranger, acquaintance or date, marital or spousal, gang rape, honor rape, rape within war, rape within the military, and trafficking. The selected narratives presented will document the ongoing historical legacy of sexual violence against women perpetrated by men. In addition, these stories will lend voice to the nature of violence perpetrated by society through the community response to the victim, as well as the deep suffering endured because of the experience of sexual violence within a rape culture.

Chapter 4 of this study presents a preliminary analysis of rape and rape culture. The term "rape" will be defined, its functions identified, and its many problematic interpretations discussed. Rape culture will be defined and social mechanisms that initiate and sanction sexual violence will be analyzed. In addition, ideological constructions that are destructive to women and perpetuate the social reproduction of sexual violence will be identified. Various theories and recent developments addressing violence against women will be explored.

4 *Introduction*

The nature of suffering for women who have experienced sexual violence will be analyzed in the fifth chapter of this study. Because victimization is perpetrated not only by the rapist but also by the rape culture, a compressed suffering of multiple feelings that interact with one another results. The inability to express pain, feelings of invisibility, isolation, shame, and self-blame work together to create an unbearable suffering that torments the victim's inner self. The Korean concept of *han* and its appropriateness to describe the multiplicity of suffering endured simultaneously by women who experience sexual violence will be explored. This chapter will go on to address the results of the continued suffering of *han* as spiritual death. A definition and analysis of spiritual death will be presented.

Chapter 6 of this study will explore the possibility for multiple spiritual resurrections for victims who have experienced a spiritual death. The traditional Korean shamanistic practice of *Han-Pu-Ri* and its ability to release *han* will be examined. In addition, the transformation from victim to survivor following spiritual resurrection will be discussed.

The seventh and final chapter will offer a summary and concluding thoughts on rape culture, spiritual violence, and visions for healing.

Notes

1 Note that I will use the term "victim" to refer to women who have experienced sexual assault. I have chosen to use this term rather than "survivor" because this study examines the spiritual death that occurs as a result of the sexual assault during a time period when, while physical survival has occurred, emotional and spiritual survival has not yet occurred.
2 Kelly Dawn Askin, *War Crimes Against Women: Prosecution in International War Crimes Tribunals* (The Hague: Kluwer Law International, 1997), p. 73, note 253.
3 Ibid., p.73. Suicide was also very common during World War II among women who feared being raped; many women kept cyanide available in case a soldier attempted to rape them. See ibid., p. 73, note 253.
4 Traci West, *Wounds of the Spirit* (New York: New York University Press, 1999), p. 55.
5 While I discuss a particular experience of rape throughout this work, I want to acknowledge that this is not the only experience. Victims have a range of experiences and should be empowered to name those experiences. Race, ethnicity, culture, religion, etc. do impact the individual's perspective and experience of sexual violence. I am not claiming a universal experience for every victim; rather, that the rape culture is manifested in particular ways throughout society and this impacts one's suffering following rape. The experience of spiritual wounding discussed in this book is based on testimony.
6 Andrew Sung Park, *From Hurt to Healing: A Theology of the Wounded* (Nashville: Abingdon Press, 2004), p. 10.
7 Beverly Lanzetta, *Radical Wisdom: A Feminist Mystical Theology* (Minneapolis: Fortress Press, 2005), p. 2.
8 Note that race, ethnicity, culture, religion, and class dividers dictate the manifestation of rape culture, which ultimately leads to the experience of *han* and spiritual death.
9 According to this myth, men are not responsible for their actions; instead, males are actually victims of their own uncontainable and instinctive nature.

2 Rape culture ordained by God?

> To tell and hear tales of terror is to wrestle demons in the night, without a compassionate God to save us.
>
> Phyllis Trible[1]

No other factor in an individual's life may be more influential than her or his religious beliefs, particularly when one experiences violence. Religion offers texts, traditions, teachings, and doctrine that convey belief systems and values that offer resources for women following a victimization. However, these resources can also act as a barrier and impede healing. As Marie Fortune and Cindy Enger explain, "it is no surprise that religious teaching and affiliation provide a significant context for many women as they address experiences of victimization ... alongside trauma of violence, a majority of women will be dealing with some aspect of religious beliefs and teachings which will serve either as a resource or a roadblock."[2]

As rape culture is found in every other aspect of life, it is also found in religion, and women often experience further victimization at the hands of their religious tradition. Multiple elements of traditional religion contribute to the prevalent rape culture. "Texts of terror"[3] have been given little attention by traditional scholars,[4] and the rape of women within biblical texts has been downplayed and sometimes dismissed completely. In some cases, violated biblical women have been blamed for their assaults, and in others the victimization of women has failed to be recognized altogether. In addition, religious traditions have participated in constructing chastity as the source of women's honor and shame. Influenced by rapes in antiquity and the tradition of female martyrdom in early Christianity, virgin martyr legends have been crafted and utilized to teach young girls and women that an intact hymen is of more value than her life.

Rape in the Bible

While the Bible offers liberating aspects, its text is fundamentally patriarchal and androcentric, presenting oppressive and damaging content. Women's experience has been excluded from biblical interpretations and oftentimes from the Bible itself. According to Letty Russell "it has become abundantly clear that the scriptures need liberation, not only from existing interpretations but also from the patriarchal bias of the texts themselves."[5] Elisabeth Schüssler Fiorenza agrees with Russell's analysis and argues that the Bible is "authored by men, written in androcentric language, reflective of male experience, selected and transmitted by male religious leadership. Without question, the Bible is a male book."[6] In addition, ethical dimensions of interpretation have been given little attention and interpreters have been unable to offer an objective and fair reading of scripture that is unaffected by identity, assumptions, social location, and personal experience.[7] Thus, the Bible is potentially harmful to women and a correlation between biblical interpretations and rape culture must be recognized. Certainly, no other single work has exerted influence over society and culture the way the Bible has. According to Cheryl Exum, the Bible has been more influential than any other document on "ideas about the place of women and about the relationships of the sexes."[8] The reading of patriarchal texts and their androcentric interpretations has influenced perceptions about women and encourages the purposeful disregard of sexual violence and women who suffer it.[9]

Rape texts and rape culture

The numerous stories of sexual violence within the Bible, as well as their traditional interpretations, have served to promote harmful ideas about women, rape, and victimization. As Exum states, "these literary rapes perpetuate ways of looking at women that encourage objectification and violence."[10] Texts have been utilized to typify how "real" rape victims behave and to demonstrate that women's claims of rape are particularly suspect. From the story of Ms. Potiphar (Genesis 39), which provides the image of a woman crying rape as one not to be trusted, to the story of Susanna (Daniel 13), which presents the notion that a rape victim should be silent, biblical texts set forth images of women and sexual violence that support rape culture. As Joy Schroeder explains,

> the lessons learned from this story [Genesis 39] warned men of the dangers posed by sexually aggressive women and to distrust women's testimony. The narrative about Susanna would make the point that women who actually *do*[11] experience sexual victimization should remain silent about their experience.[12]

In multiple texts, threats of sexual violence against women are ignored altogether in favor of focusing on threats to men. For instance, in Genesis 19 Lot's daughters are threatened with rape. While the threat of the angels being violated by the Sodomites is fully recognized, Lot's offer of his virgin daughters to the angry mob and the threat the women faced have been given little attention. Likewise, in what have become known as the wife–sister incidents,[13] both Sarah (Genesis 12, 20) and Rebecca (Genesis 26) are threatened with rape when they are told to present themselves as sisters rather than wives to their husbands. Although these texts have been analyzed for their similar characteristics and foreshadowing of events among other elements, serious discussions regarding the threats of sexual violence against Sarah and Rebecca are virtually missing.

While some biblical instances that recount sexual violence have been called rape, others have been promulgated as incidents that reflect the historical culture but are unworthy of the classification of rape. Others have been ignored altogether. Rape culture is ever present in the exegeses of these texts. Whereas some androcentric interpreters have refused to discuss the topic of rape and instead relegated it to discussions about marriage customs and family life,[14] others have addressed and analyzed rape texts, offering interpretations that blame the woman for both the sexual assault and the outcome following her victimization. Some interpreters have chosen to focus their analyses on the men in the text and dismiss the woman's victimization completely. Thus, interpretations of biblical rape texts fully participate in the existing rape culture and function to support dismissive attitudes and further victimization of women who have suffered sexual violence.

The rape of Dinah (Genesis 34), the rape of the unnamed pilegesh[15] (Judges 19), and the rape of Tamar (2 Samuel 13) have commonly been recognized as the "rape texts" of the Bible. In what follows I will discuss each of these texts and identify how they have been utilized to perpetuate rape culture. In addition, I will examine 2 Samuel 16:22, a text that describes the violent rape of David's ten pilegesh. While it has been largely overlooked as a "text of terror," its brutality demands attention.

The rape of Dinah

> Now Dinah the daughter of Leah, whom she had borne to Jacob, went out to visit the women of the region. When Shechem son of Hamor the Hivite, prince of the region, saw her, he seized her and lay with her by force. And his soul was drawn to Dinah daughter of Jacob; he loved the girl, and spoke tenderly to her.
>
> (Genesis 34:1–3)[16]

In Genesis 34, Dinah, the daughter of Leah and Jacob, is raped by Shechem when she leaves her home to visit women in her community. Following the rape, Shechem wants to marry Dinah, claiming to love her. Jacob and Dinah's brothers agree to the marriage if Shechem and his men agree to be circumcised. Once the circumcisions have taken place, Dinah's brothers attack the men and slaughter them all, abducting the women and children of the city. When Jacob condemns his son's actions, they ask if they should have allowed their sister to be treated like a whore.

First, it is important to note that the text itself is problematic. As Fortune points out,

> At no point is the reader provided with any information about Dinah's experience or reaction to the assault. Neither are we provided with any information about Dinah's life afterwards. Since she lost her virginity and her potential husband was killed by her brothers, what man would have her? And without a man to provide for her, what would happen to her?[17]

Dinah has no voice; although she is sexually violated, the author focuses on how this impacts the men in the story. It offers a male perspective, focuses on male experience, and presents male bias.

According to Susan Scholz, "The story of Dinah is one of the most contested rape stories in the Hebrew Bible. During its extensive history of interpretation, Jewish and Christian interpreters mainly ignore Dinah."[18] The exegetical focus of Genesis 34 has been the men of the story, the tribal connotations, literary–historical composition, etc. George Coats has entitled his chapter addressing Genesis 34 "The Rape of Shechem" and states the narrative is "a simple plot focused *not*[19] on the rape of Dinah by Shechem, but on the rape of Shechem by the brothers of Dinah."[20] Stuart West also focuses on Shechem, stating that this narrative recounts the "conquest of Shechem" as "a symbol for the future conquest of the land of Canaan."[21] He goes on to discuss Shechem in a positive light, stating that he "was man enough to do the 'right' thing by offering to marry her."[22] Calum Carmichael designates Genesis 34 as the "Shechem story" and argues that it "is written up in such a way as to reveal a profound tension of viewpoints between Jacob and his two sons."[23]

Focusing on marriage rituals, John Otwell centers on Shechem not following traditional wedding customs; although he acknowledges Shechem as a legitimate bridegroom.[24] Tikva Frymer-Kensky also focuses on Shechem's ignoring the marriage customs of his time by not obtaining parental consent before intercourse. She states that "Shechem never intended any harm," and explains that Dinah's point of view is not material since the right of consent did not belong to women and girls who were unwed.[25] Lyn M. Bechtel favors this line of thought and argues that the issue of this text does not center on whether or not a rape occurred, but rather on whether or not the intercourse between Shechem and Dinah was considered "shameful" within the group-oriented society. She claims that because Shechem tried to repair the situation and his "overall action ... is one of honor ... there is no indication that Dinah is raped. The description of Shechem's behavior and attitude does not fit that of a rapist."[26]

Other traditional interpreters who have given attention to Dinah have claimed that her actions were unwise and dangerous.[27] Some have zeroed in on Dinah's attempted visit as cause for her rape and the massacre of Shechem and his men. For instance, G.C. Aalders states:

> We can surmise that [Dinah] also had some natural desires to be seen by the young men of the city as well ... It was disturbing that Dinah would so flippantly expose herself to the men of this pagan city ... As a matter of fact, Dinah was far more at fault for what had happened than anyone else in the City of Shechem.[28]

Likewise, Carmichael claims that Dinah had given "some indication that she was willing ... she took it upon herself to go out and visit the women of the area, and when Shechem encountered her, he, a prince, treated her with great tenderness." He also states that, unlike Dinah, her brothers have "a very high sexual standard."[29]

Thus, in multiple cases, traditional commentators and their interpretations lack a hermeneutical ethic[30] and instead employ assumptions and experience influenced by rape culture to analyze the text. In doing so, these commentators have participated in rape culture by blaming and silencing Dinah, disregarding her point of view. In addition, this text is clearly androcentric in that the focus of the narrative is the men and their reactions rather than the rape; Dinah, who has been sexually violated, is silent. Thus, both biblical interpreters and the biblical narrator have ignored Dinah.

The rape of the unnamed pilegesh

> "Here are my virgin daughter and his concubine; let me bring them out now. Ravish them and do whatever you want to them; but against this man do not do such a vile thing." But the men would not listen to him. So the man seized his concubine, and put her out to them. They wantonly raped her, and abused her all through the night until the morning.
> (Judges 19:24–25)

Judges 19 relates the story of an unnamed pilegesh brutally gang-raped throughout the night by a mob of Benjaminite men from Gibeah when her husband, the Levite, hands her over to them in order to save himself from being sexually assaulted. She was then dismembered, limb by limb, into twelve pieces by her husband.[31] According to Exum, "The gang rape of the unnamed wife of an unnamed Levite by unnamed members of a mob of ruffians recounted in Chapter 19 of the book of Judges ... is perhaps the most gruesome and violent tale in the Bible."[32]

According to Exum, this particular rape text is a clear example of a phallocentric narrative that encourages objectification and violence against women. It is not a historical report of an actual event; rather, it is a literary creation that presents a woman being "raped by the pen" and "is brutally excessive and offensive."[33] The woman is never named and has no voice, encouraging the reader to disregard her as a person. In addition, the woman is a pilegesh, commonly translated as "concubine" or a wife of second rank, which Exum argues is purposeful to "give the impression that she is less valued, and probably more expendable than a legitimate wife."[34] The dismemberment of the pilegesh functions to desexualize her symbolically "by violently opening up the mystery of woman and diffusing her threat by scattering her parts."[35] Furthermore, the text is constructed in such a way that it spirals into a series of violence; the story of the rape of the pilegesh culminates in full-scale war. Thus, the strategy of the narrator is to scapegoat the woman in an effort to blame her for violence and disorder. According to Exum, this narrative was crafted as a narrative punishment of a woman for her exercising her own sexual freedom;[36] no other reason can explain the need for its extreme and violent nature.[37]

Although the rape of the unnamed pilegesh in Judges 19 is widely accepted as a rape text among biblical scholars, the lack of interpretation of this text is representative of rape culture. Judges 19, in its horrific and violent nature, has been particularly troublesome for readers and interpreters. However, until recently, the rape of the unnamed pilegesh received little attention because it was considered merely part of an appendix that extends from chapter 17 to 21. The gang-rape and dismemberment of a woman seemed undeserving of attention. According to Tammi Schneider,

> Despite the importance of this story for understanding Judges, scholarship in general has not focused attention on this chapter. Perhaps the absence of a judge makes it uninteresting. Perhaps it is too painful. Perhaps it does not fit well with the military hero worship of many commentaries on this book.[38]

Feminist commentators, deeply disturbed by this rape narrative, exposed its horrific nature, arguing that although we would like to forget it, we are "commanded to speak it."[39] As Phyllis Trible notes, this text "depicts the horror of male power, brutality, and triumphalism; of female helplessness, abuse, and annihilation. To hear this story is to inhabit a world of unrelenting terror that refuses to let us pass by on the other side."[40]

The rape of Tamar

> But when she brought them near him to eat, he took hold of her, and said to her, "Come, lie with me, my sister." She answered him, "No, my brother, do not force me; for such a thing is not done in Israel; do not do anything so vile! As for me, where could I carry my shame? And as for you, you would be as one of the scoundrels in Israel. Now therefore, I beg you, speak to the king; for he will not withhold me from you."

But he would not listen to her; and being stronger than she was, he forced her to lay with him.

(2 Samuel 13:11–14)

A story of rape and incest emerges in 2 Samuel 13 when Amnon, son of King David, decides that he "loves" his sister Tamar. He devises a plan with his friend Jonadab, pretends he is ill, and asks David to send Tamar with food for him. David agrees and once Tamar is alone with Amnon he propositions her; she rejects his advances and begs him to marry her first. However, Amnon refuses and rapes her. Following the rape, Amnon despises Tamar. Tamar tells her brother Absalom that Amnon raped her and he tells her to be silent. When David hears of the rape, he is angry with Amnon, but does not punish him because Amnon was his firstborn and he loves him (13:21). Eventually, Absalom avenges his sister and murders Amnon. Tamar lives the rest of her life as "a desolate woman in her brother Absalom's house" (13:20).

According to Scholz, "If there is a quintessential rape story in the Hebrew Bible, it is the story of Tamar."[41] Many scholars have recognized the text as such and denounced Amnon's actions. However, as Schroeder explains,

> through the centuries, readers are repeatedly drawn to the same questions: Why did Tamar beg Amnon to ask David to marry her when the Law of Moses clearly forbade marriage between brother and sister? Why did Amnon's love turn to hate after he raped her? Why did Tamar say that Amnon's act of throwing her out of the house was worse than his act of rape? Finally, why did David not punish Amnon?[42]

In response to these questions, some commentators have recognized the public shame and loss of marriage prospects that Tamar would have faced as a result of being raped. However, others have completely underestimated the social consequences for rape victims and have claimed that Tamar invited Amnon to rape her.[43]

According to Pamela Tamarkin Reis, Amnon is not guilty of rape; rather, Tamar is to blame for her victimization. Reis claims that Tamar invites "sexual intimacy ... by her easy virtue, persistent ambition, and implacable stupidity."[44] She further asserts that Tamar demonstrates an interest in Amnon by baking cakes in the shape of hearts, not attempting to run when Amnon tells her to come to him – instead going to his bedside to "flirt" – and resisting only when she realizes that Amnon wants to have intercourse. Reis states that Tamar "submits to intercourse without attempting to call out."[45] Thus, Reis rejects the "rape verdict" due to "the tell-tale heart-cakes, Tamar's willingness to be alone with a man, and her failure to call out."[46]

Reis's interpretation of this text is a clear example of rape culture. Her claim that Tamar is responsible for her rape reinforces androcentric attitudes that are accepted as norms. In addition to victim blaming, Reis denies Tamar's right to refuse to consent to intercourse as well as Amnon's responsibility to acknowledge and respect Tamar's opposition. This interpretation makes the claim that Amnon is not responsible for his actions, reinforcing the classic myth of the uncontrollable male sexual drive.[47] Reis lacks a hermeneutical ethic; she is unable to offer an objective and fair reading of this text due to her own preconceived notions that have been influenced by rape culture.

The rape of David's pilegesh

> Ahithophel said to Absalom, "Go into your father's concubines, the ones he has left to look after the house; and all Israel will hear that you have made yourself odious to your father, and the hands of all who are with you will be strengthened." So they pitched a tent for Absalom upon the roof; and Absalom went in to his father's concubines in the sight of all Israel.
> (2 Samuel 16:21–22)

2 Samuel 16:22 presents the terror experienced by ten pilegesh who are dragged upon a roof and raped "in the sight of all Israel" as a political coup to overthrow David as king. Absalom, David's son is directed by Ahithophel, who was thought to be an oracle of God, to "go into" his father's pilegesh in order to claim the throne. Ultimately, Absalom fails to steal the kingship from David and is killed in battle. David locks away the pilegesh to live as widows for the rest of their days.

This particular text is problematic on many levels. First, the text itself silences the women and offers them little acknowledgement; they do not speak, they are not named, they are simply objects in a narrative receiving an action. In addition, the sexual violence endured by these women has been largely ignored within scholarship. While traditional commentators have examined nearly every aspect of this biblical verse, the ten women who became pawns within a military strategy and were brutally raped have received little attention within interpretations of this text.

The story of the sexual violation of the ten pilegesh has never been acknowledged as a rape narrative due to assumptions made by biblical scholars that sexual practices are presupposed by the story. "It is usually suggested that there must have been a custom whereby a successor to the throne takes as his own the harem of a previous king."[48] Thus, the argument follows that if a man takes or has intercourse with the king's harem, he claims the throne.[49] Agreeing with this argument, in describing Absalom's rape of the pilegesh, David Gunn has claimed that it is a formal act,[50] whereas Gerhard von Rad argues that it is "a symbolic action intended to gain the confidence of the people for Absalom."[51] According to Gnana Robinson, "this action will affirm in the eyes of the public that Absalom has asserted his rights as king."[52] Consequently, the ten pilegesh being dragged upon a roof so that Absalom could "go into" them "in the sight of all Israel" is not considered a rape, but rather a political coup.

Eugene Peterson describes the rape as a "public relations" event to establish Absalom as David's replacement, and that served to "arouse the imaginations" of the people:

> The first element is sheer public relations: Absalom is to enter his father's harem and sleep with the concubines. This would dramatically establish Absalom's replacement of David in the public mind ... The event was to be staged so that no one in Jerusalem would miss either the act or its significance. And so Absalom orders a tent to be pitched on the palace roof – everyone in the streets watches the concubines file in, followed by Absalom. The tent, while preventing people from actually seeing him in bed with the women, also served to arouse the imaginations of everyone gathered around ... what goes on in the minds of the crowds who look at the tent from the outside far exceeds what actually takes place inside ... looking at the tent and listening for the sounds coming from it is everyone's occupation. The longer Absalom is in the tent, the more his reputation grows ... All Absalom has to do is indulge himself sexually with the concubines while Ahithophel gets rid of David.[53]

Peterson's interpretation of this text is troublesome, to say the least. While he claims this narrative describes a political coup, Peterson takes many liberties with the text that have no basis. Although there is no statement in the biblical text that describes how the pilegesh arrived on the roof, he presents the women as "filing in" – as if they were willing participants in Absalom's act. In addition, he turns the victimization of ten women into a pornographic scene with voyeurs straining to hear sexual murmurs, and quite possibly violent cries, coming from the tent. Peterson even describes the thoughts of those in the crowd, claiming that their imaginations had gotten the best of them. He describes Absalom as "indulging" in the act, but never addresses the women's reaction to their victimization.

Other commentators, while acknowledging that Absalom is attempting to overthrow David under Ahithophel's guidance, also state that the act is problematic. According to A.A. Anderson and Ernst Wurthwein, it is highly unlikely that Absalom's act would have resulted in legitimating a claim to the king's throne.[54] Anderson states:

> the cohabitation with the concubines of David may not have given Absalom any special legal claim to the kingship; it is doubtful that this act could add anything to what was already given by the divine choice and popular acclamation ... this cohabitation ... was a deliberate deception to give the impression to the people in general that David was actually dead ... it was forbidden for a son to take his father's wife, at least while the father was alive.[55]

Deuteronomy 22:30 states: "A man shall not marry his father's wife, thereby violating his father's rights." Thus, what can be inferred from Anderson's statement is that rather than Absalom's act being a formal way to claim the kingship, he violated law by raping his father's pilegesh in order to deceive the people into believing David was dead and that he, Absalom, was the new king.

When reading this text from its historical context, an analysis of the textual clues alongside the social and cultural world reveals that Absalom did in fact rape the ten pilegesh. During this time period rape was understood as the theft of another man's sexual property; rape was a crime committed against the man who owned the woman, not against the woman herself (Deuteronomy 22:22–25).[56] Thus, in this particular situation, the pilegesh are considered as belonging to David. Absalom entered the sexual property not only of another man, but of his father, violating two laws. Consequently, a rape, as legally defined, did occur.

It also must be noted that Absalom failed in his attempt to seize the throne. The rape of these ten women was not divinely ordained, as Ahithophel had claimed. The fact that Absalom did not successfully steal the kingship is evidence that his actions were wrong. After raping the women David was still king and the women still belonged to David. Thus, because Absalom had sexual intercourse with another man's wives, he had committed rape.

The text is clear that the pilegesh did not consent to intercourse with Absalom. Had they consented, the pilegesh would have been punished as the law required of an adulteress (Deuteronomy 22:22): they would have been stoned to death. Instead, these women are punished by David: they are locked away as widows for the rest of their days; not because they had done any wrong, but because David no longer wanted anything to do with the pilegesh who had been defiled by his son and were a reminder of Absalom's revolt against him. Hence, claims that 2 Samuel 16:21–22 is not a rape text based on historical cultural context are wrong.

What this text presents is an early example of rape as a weapon of war; however, the brutality against the women has been ignored and instead the narrative has been examined as a political coup by a son against his father. This is problematic on many levels and functions to support the existing rape culture where attitudes and practices condone and excuse sexual violence. The idea that this text simply describes a political coup and thus that the violence perpetrated against the women need not be acknowledged supports this culture.

Granted, the word utilized in this particular text to denote the rape is bô, meaning to enter, and is different from the language[57] utilized in those texts that are considered rape narratives. However, this is because rape within war was considered an unavoidable occurrence. The nature of rape within war was thought to be different from the nature of rape that occurred within daily life. This is comparable to attitudes that prevail today. Until recently, rape within war was not considered a war crime. In addition, it is only recently that the use of rape as a weapon of war has been prosecuted.[58] This does not mean that rape was not or is not occurring during war; rather, that it has been considered a consequence of war and thus ignored, just as it is in this biblical text.

As Exum describes Judges 19, this is also a phallocentric text that focuses on the actions and views of the male characters. According to Stone: "The text describes male interests, presenting events from a perspective that is concerned almost exclusively with the male participants in sexual practice."[59] Just as traditional commentators failed to address the rape of the unnamed pilegesh in Judges, traditional commentators have failed to address the rape of David's ten pilegesh. Because this text has been characterized as a political coup and part of a larger narrative, the violent rape has been ignored. This failure to acknowledge the brutal victimization of the ten pilegesh is harmful to women, encourages the purposeful disregard of sexual violence, and is representative of the prevailing rape culture.

Purity legends

For centuries, the Christian tradition has recounted stories of saintly women heroic for sacrificing their lives in order to preserve their virginity. Influenced by the historical reports of Christian women imprisoned, martyred, and often raped by the authorities of the Roman Empire, the Church began to tell tales of women who protected their purity through either divine or providential intervention or giving their lives. Often these legends presented the victim as having a choice between submitting to sexual intercourse or capitulating to death. According to Schroeder, "In many Christian imaginations, the pure – but dead – virgin martyr contrasts with the tragic survivor of rape, who invited and enjoyed her sexual attack."[60]

Girls are raised from a young age learning the legends of women who have been canonized saints and labeled heroic for giving up their lives in order to protect their chastity. Female sexual suffering is valorized and the cultural paradigms of virginity and martyrdom have severely impacted gender identity, construction of sexuality, and life experience of women. Women's sexuality is associated with virginity and motherhood while women's sense of morality is associated with sexual shame. In this section I will examine the rape of Lucretia, a story that has greatly influenced the idea of chastity as a source of honor and shame. In addition, I will explore the legend of the virgin martyrs and will give special attention to Saint Maria Goretti.

The rape of Lucretia

The rape and suicide of the Roman matron Lucretia well demonstrates the idea of chastity as a source of honor and the public and private shame that occurs as a result of experiencing sexual violence. The legend begins with Lucretia's husband, Collatinus, claiming the prize of having the wife with the most womanly virtues. The defeated Sextus Tarquinius was "seized with wicked desire to debauch Lucretia by force; not only her beauty, but her proved chastity as well, provoked him."[61] He went to the sleeping Lucretia and awoke her, telling her to be still, that his sword was in his hand and he would murder her if she uttered a word. Unmoved by the fear of death, Lucretia refused to submit. However, Tarquinius then threatened her with disgrace, "saying that when she was dead he would kill his slave and leave him naked beside her, that she might be said to have been put to death in adultery with a man of base condition."[62] With this threat, Lucretia relented and Tarquinius raped her.

Following the rape, Lucretia summoned her husband and father to tell them how she had been violated and demanded that they vow revenge. Lucretia then said: "As for me, I am innocent of fault, but I will take my punishment. Never shall Lucretia provide a precedent for unchaste women to escape what they deserve."[63] She then took a knife from under her robe and stabbed herself through the heart; suicide was the only means of redeeming her honor.

Within Roman tradition, the idea that women desired to be raped was firmly entrenched in society. In addition, "pollution caused by rape or adultery was essentially a religious matter, affecting the woman and her immediate family in a deeper and continuing way."[64] Pre-emptive suicide was understood as the only possible means to redeem the woman's honor and virtue. Ian Donaldson explains, "Like a religious sacrifice, the suicide seems to cleanse the effects of pollution, and to restore lost purity and innocence."[65] Thus, although Lucretia was considered guiltless by Roman historians commenting on this story, her suicide was praised as honorable and the main element that proved her innocence.

Jerome and Tertullian also commended Lucretia's taking of her own life. According to Tertullian, while Lucretia did not have the same high morals that inspire Christian women to commit suicide if raped, she was still a "virtuous heathen whose example might be remembered and emulated by Christians."[66] Jerome also cites Lucretia as an example for Christian women. In fact, he claims that rape is the exception to all restrictions against suicide. He states, "It is not man's prerogative to lay violent hands upon himself, but rather to freely receive death from others. In persecutions it is not lawful to commit suicide except when one's chastity is jeopardized."[67] In fact, Jerome claims that, "Although God is able to do all things, he cannot raise up a virgin after a fall."[68] Despite the fact that every affliction and mutilation would be healed at the time of the resurrection of the body, according to Jerome, even divine power could not restore a broken hymen.

This being said, Lucretia's innocence has also been questioned by some Christian interpreters. For instance, Augustine denounced the act of suicide and blamed Lucretia for her rape. He argued that suicide proved that she was culpable, claiming she would not have taken such action had she not felt guilt. He writes, "If she is adulterous, why is she praised? If chaste, why was she put to death?"[69]

The rape of Lucretia is a crucial text in that it represents the Roman tradition of a woman's honor and shame being dictated by her chastity.

In addition, it is foundational to the Christian ideal of a woman's purity being connected to her relationship with God and the continued societal notion that rape is a fate worse than death. Jerome's and Tertullian's comments are devastating and reinforce the rape victim's fear that a life after sexual violence is one consumed by dishonor and shame and not worth living. While Augustine argues against suicide, he does so by blaming Lucretia and calling her guilty. In doing so, he participates in rape culture and supports the myth of women being inherently sexual beings who desire to be raped.[70]

Women and Christian martyrdom

During early Christian history women were among those Christians who were persecuted under Roman rule. Sexual violence against female captives was sanctioned as it was "impious" to execute a virgin. Suetonius explains, "Since ancient usage made it impious to strangle maidens, young girls were first violated by the executioner and then strangled."[71] In addition, Schroeder explains that ancient literature confirms that sexual violence was inflicted on prisoners as a form of entertainment in the amphitheater. An imprisoned woman who is forced to perform sexual acts in the theater is mentioned by Pseudo-Lucian in his work *The Ass*.[72] The suffering of sexual violence by women as a form of persecution was acknowledged by the early Church. Tertullian and Clement commented on rape as part of women's experience of martyrdom.[73] Both commended women for their courage, and Tertullian argued that a woman condemned to a brothel was acknowledgement that chastity was valued by Christian women.

> Crucify us! Torture us! Condemn us! Degrade us! … by condemning a Christian woman to the pimp rather than to the lion you believed and admitted that among us a stain upon virtue is considered more terrible than any punishment or any death.[74]

Thus, the focus on sexual violence and Christian martyrdom reinforced ideas that a woman's chastity is more valuable than her life and in some cases convinced women to sacrifice their lives in order to protect their virginity. In addition, it influenced Christianity and resulted in the development of rape threat narratives with divine or providential intervention and the virgin martyr legends.

Rape threat narratives and divine/providential intervention

Early and medieval church literature includes multiple narratives describing the miraculous rescue of a virgin from rape. Two frequent themes that appear are divine intervention and divine providence. Dramatic tactics come into play in narratives that claim divine intervention, including "devices such as thunderbolts, angels, and giant serpents. These awe-inspiring occurrences make God's power and the woman's chastity manifest to believers and unbelievers alike."[75] Providential intervention often appears in narratives in the form of human actions, "but these actions are providential because God is at work through them."[76]

The act of divine intervention is clearly demonstrated in the Acts of Peter. In this text, a narrative about the attempted rape of the apostle Peter's ten-year-old daughter is presented. It states that, because of her beauty, many men lusted after the young girl. She was abducted by Ptolemy for "corruption and shame"; however, God intervened, striking her with paralysis so that she would be unattractive. Ptolemy returned the girl to Peter and although Peter had the ability to heal his daughter, he chose not to do so in order to ensure that she would not cause lust in any other men. Although Peter's daughter is left in a disfigured state,

> Ptolemy who is blinded by tears of repentance and wants to commit suicide … is made whole again by divine intervention and becomes a true believer – one who sees with the eyes of his flesh and the eyes of his soul – and is finally portrayed as both a spiritual and material benefactor of the Christian community.[77]

This text is unquestionably harmful towards women. While in some texts miraculous intervention occurs in the form of striking the perpetrator, here the young girl is struck by the divine with paralysis to curb her beauty. Although Peter can heal his daughter, he does not, explaining that if his daughter remains in her God-given state, men will not be tempted to commit unholy acts against her. Thus, rather than place responsibility on Ptolemy for abducting his daughter with the intent to defile her, Peter blames his daughter for her attempted rape. In addition, instead of being punished, Ptolemy is "made whole again." The young girl is victimized by Ptolemy, Peter, and God. She is held responsible for Ptolemy's conduct, while Ptolemy is rewarded by God. Essentially, this text makes the claim that God punishes rape victims and rewards rapists.

The *Acts of Paul and Thecla* offers a narrative that demonstrates providential intervention on Thecla's behalf. When attacked by a man named Alexander, Thecla first calls out for Paul; however, when she realizes he is not there to help her, she successfully defends herself. "She ripped his cloak, took the wreath from his head and made him a laughingstock."[78] Infuriated, Alexander brings Thecla before the proconsul and has her "condemned to the beasts." Realizing the threat of rape she will face if she is imprisoned, Thecla petitions the pro-consul, asking "that she might remain pure until she was to fight against the beasts."[79] Tryphaena, a noble woman, intervenes and takes Thecla into her home to protect her chastity.

This text is an important narrative because it presents Thecla and Tryphaena as active agents in safeguarding Thecla from rape. Divine providence is at work through the actions of both women. This being said, Thecla's chastity is of more concern than her facing death. Her virginity remaining intact is the crucial point of the narrative. Schroeder explains that,

> Thecla's authority emanates from her relationship with the deity. The narrative seeks to portray God's providence and the authority given to male and female believers. This authority is related to the believer's chastity ... Power resides in the woman because of her unbroken hymen and her resolution to remain chaste.[80]

Consequently, while the women acting as active agents is an important element that must be recognized in this narrative, the message of chastity first overpowers the text and reinforces the notion that a woman's purity is more precious than her life.

The legend of the virgin martyr

The legend of the virgin martyr developed from the tradition of women's martyrdom in early Christianity. Within these legends, women who martyred themselves to remain chaste not only laid down their lives but also suffered gruesome and torturous deaths in order to protect their purity "for Jesus, their heavenly spouse."[81] For instance, Saints Margaret and Cecilia were boiled; Saint Agnes was beheaded; Saint Katherine was mangled by spiked wheels; Saints Agatha and Barbara both had their breasts torn from their bodies; and Saint Apollonia had her teeth wrenched out. Saint Ursula was butchered in a mass martyrdom along with eleven thousand other virgins and Saint Lucy gouged out her own eyes to discourage any man from being tempted by her.[82] "The saint's torture was typically directed to the femaleness of the victim, reflecting the elements of sadism or pornography in the legend."[83] Each of these women demonstrated her love for God through her horrific death, which occurred with her hymen intact. As a result, they were all elevated to sainthood and are celebrated as the virgin martyrs in Catholic tradition.

The historicity of many virgin martyrs has been seriously challenged due to elements of their legends remaining the same.[84] As Schroeder explains, "a woman is brought before the authorities because of her refusal to marry or her refusal to worship the pagan gods; her chastity is threatened but never violated; she dies a martyr's death; she is assured a heavenly reward for her faithfulness to Christ her bridegroom."[85] Similarity among these legends was deliberate as the virgin martyr genre sought to "suppress individualizing detail and to bring out the saints' resemblance to one another and to Christ."[86]

The virgin martyr legend and the Christian concept of elevating a woman to heroic and saintly status as a result are problematic in that they support violence against women and serve to reinforce rape culture. These legends and their claims that a woman's chastity is valued over her life are androcentric in nature and damaging to women. Susan Brownmiller explains,

> Through legend and lore, history has mythified not the strong woman who defends herself successfully against bodily assault, but the beautiful woman who dies a violent death while trying. A good heroine is a dead heroine ... the sacrifice of life, we learn, is the most perfect testament to a woman's integrity.[87]

The legend of Saint Maria Goretti

The legend of Maria Goretti deserves special attention due to its unique position and recent evolution. Having occurred in 1902 in Italy, many of the elements of Maria's story have been confirmed, unlike those of other virgin martyr legends. At the age of twelve she was attacked by a farmhand named Alessandro Serenelli, who demanded that she submit to his raping her or sacrifice her life. Refusing to be sexually violated, Maria accepted death: Serenelli stabbed her fourteen times while Maria accepted his repeated blows, never raising a hand to defend herself. As she lay dying she used her last breaths to apologize to her mother for upsetting her and to forgive Serenelli for snuffing out her young life.

Serenelli confessed to Maria's murder, explaining that he had given her every opportunity to submit to his rape. During his prison sentence he claimed that Maria came to him in a vision dressed in white and holding flowers, convincing him to repent. After serving twenty-seven years, Serenelli went to Maria's mother to apologize and she forgave him. He spent the rest of his days living with an order of monks.

Maria became a mythic figure almost instantly and, as a result of her protected chastity, she was canonized a saint by the Catholic Church in 1950, just forty-eight years after her death.[88] Serenelli was present at the side of Maria's mother and other family members for the event, which attracted the largest crowd recorded at that time to St. Peter's Square. At her canonization, Pope Pius XII referred to Maria's life-threatening rape as "an attractive pleasure," stating: "From Maria's story carefree children and young people with their zest for life can learn not to be led astray by attractive pleasures which are not only ephemeral and empty, but also sinful."[89]

This modern legend of Maria's virgin martyrdom well demonstrates rape culture at work. It has been and still is utilized to regulate the lives of and condone violence against women. As Kathleen Zuanich Young explains,

> The institutionalization of violence (and male dominance) in the Catholic Church is accomplished through the handing on of stories of virgin martyrs as one facet of the social control of women, their sexuality and their bodies. Maria Goretti is a modern mythic figure, with many levels of meaning to the myth.[90]

Maria's legend claims that she "chose" a horrific death because her Catholic upbringing taught her that her chastity was more valuable than her life. In addition, "had Alessandro Serenelli gone through with his intentions, Maria's death would have amounted to a futile gesture, canonically speaking."[91] The legend's emphasis on Maria's non-reactive submission to her death and the claim that she used her last breaths to apologize to her mother and forgive her murderer support the socio-cultural ideal that women must be passive, apologetic, and forgiving, regardless of the level of wrong committed against them. As Young explains, "the rape victim, the sexually abused girl, and the battered wife are given a message ... to take responsibility for their abusers, to forgive them, and by forgiving them, redeem them."[92] The pope's use of the phrase "attractive pleasure" to describe Maria's harrowing attack not only demonstrates the cultural tendency to confuse rape with sex rather than recognize it as a brutal exercise of power and control,[93] but truly epitomizes the nature of rape culture: the notion that women want to be raped and men bear no responsibility.

Conclusion

While religion can offer resources for women, traditions can also be very troublesome, damaging towards women, and a major obstacle for the healing process. Many religious texts and traditions are androcentric and perpetuate the current rape culture. In addition, interpretations of texts and events lack a hermeneutical ethic and employ patriarchal assumptions. The interpretations discussed are not without bias; rather, they clearly infuse misogynistic elements into their analyses as a result of socio-cultural influence.

The tradition of chastity as women's honor and shame and its adaptation to Christianity fuel societal notions that women who are raped have lost integrity and sullied their relationship with God. Legends of virgin martyrs and their pornographic torture are disturbing and, according to Young, "are used as a kind of sexual terrorism."[94] They are taught with the intent of conditioning women and girls to believe that there is no worse thing in life that could happen to them than being raped: having your breasts ripped from your body, being boiled in a vat of oil, and being butchered or beheaded cannot equate to the suffering endured as a result of the dishonor and shame of being raped.

Notes

1 Phyllis Trible, *Texts of Terror: Literary-Feminist Readings of Biblical Narratives* (Philadelphia: Fortress Press, 1984), p. 4.
2 Marie Fortune and Cindy Enger, "Violence against Women and the Role of Religion." The National Online Resource Center on Violence against Women. Retrieved from: http://www.vawnet.org/applied-research-papers/print-document.php?doc_id=411, par 1, 3.
3 Trible.
4 Throughout this work, I will use the phrase "traditional scholar" to refer to commentators who do not offer a feminist approach in their interpretations.

5 Letty Russell, "Authority and the Challenge of Feminist Interpretations," in Letty Russell, ed., Feminist Interpretation of the Bible (Philadelphia: Westminster, 1985), p. 85.
6 Elisabeth Schüssler Fiorenza, "The Will to Choose or to Reject," in Russell, ed., p. 130.
7 See Charles Cosgrove, ed., *The Meanings We Choose: Hermeneutical Ethics, Indeterminacy, and the Conflict of Interpretation* (New York: T&T Clark International, 2004).
8 Cheryl Exum, "Feminist Criticism: Whose Interests are Being Served?," in Gale A. Yee, ed., *Judges and Method: New Approaches in Biblical Studies* (Minneapolis: Fortress Press, 1995). Also see Vincent L. Wimbush, "Biblical–Historical Study as Liberation: Toward an Afro-Christian Hermeneutic." *Journal of Religious Thought* 42(2) (Fall–Winter 1985–1986): pp. 9–21; The Bible and Culture Collective, *The Postmodern Bible* (New Haven: Yale University Press, 1995), p. 1.
9 For additional information about scripture and sexual violence, see Marie Fortune, *Sexual Violence: The Unmentionable Sin* (New York: The Pilgrim Press, 1983).
10 Cheryl Exum, "Raped by the Pen," in *Fragmented Women: Feminist Subversions of Biblical Narratives. Journal for the Study of the Old Testament Supplement Series* 163 (Valley Forge: Trinity Press International, 1993), p. 170.
11 My italics.
12 Joy Schroeder, *Dinah's Lament: The Biblical Legacy of Sexual Violence in Christian Interpretation* (Minneapolis: Fortress Press, 2007), p. 193.
13 See David Carr, *Reading the Fractures of Genesis: Historical and Literary Approaches* (Louisville: Westminster John Knox Press, 1996); Danna Fewell, *Reading Between Texts: Intertextuality and the Hebrew Bible* (Louisville: Westminster John Knox Press, 1992); André Wénin, *Studies in the Book of Genesis: Literature, Redaction and History* (Leuven: Leuven University Press, 2001).
14 For instance, see Johannes Pedersen, *Israel: Its Life and Culture.* 2 vols (London: Oxford University Press, 1959). Pedersen discusses rape under the topics of appropriate and inappropriate marriage arrangements and incest prohibition.
15 Pilegesh is commonly translated to concubine or wife of second rank.
16 Note that all biblical quotes will be taken from the New Revised Standard Version unless otherwise stated.
17 Fortune, p. 51.
18 Susan Scholz, *Sacred Witness: Rape in the Hebrew Bible* (Minneapolis: Fortress Press, 2010), p. 32.
19 My italics.
20 George W. Coats, *Genesis with an Introduction to Narrative Literature.* Vol. 1 (Grand Rapids: Eerdmans, 1983), p. 234.
21 Stuart West, "The Rape of Dinah and the Conquest of Shechem." *Dor le Dor* 8(3) (Spring, 1980): p. 151.
22 Ibid., p. 158.
23 Calum Carmichael, *Women, Law, and the Genesis Traditions* (Edinburgh: Edinburgh University Press, 1979), p. 33.
24 John Otwell, *And Sarah Laughed: The Status of Women in the Old Testament* (Philadelphia: Westminster Press, 1977), p. 37.
25 Tikva Frymer-Kensky, "Virginity in the Bible," in Victor Matthews, Bernard Levinson, and Tikva Frymer-Kensky, eds., *Gender and Law in the Hebrew Bible and the Ancient Near East.* (Sheffield: Sheffield Academic Press, 1998), pp. 79–96, 86.
26 Lyn M. Bechtel, "What if Dinah is not Raped? (Genesis 34)." *Journal for the Study of the Old Testament* 62 (1994): pp. 19–36, 31.
27 See Genesis Rabbah LXXX:II h–I, III f–g in Bernard of Clairvaux, *Selected Works* (New York: Paulist Press, 1987 [written 1125]), p. 124; Ancrene Wisse, *Anchoritic Spirituality* (New York: Paulist Press, 1991 [written 1200–1230]), p. 68;

J. Calvin, *A Commentary on Genesis* (London: Banner of Truth, 1965 [written 1554]), p. 218.
28 G.C. Aalders, Genesis. Vol. 2 (Grand Rapids: Zondervan, 1981), pp. 154, 159.
29 Carmichael, p. 42.
30 For more information of hermeneutical ethics, see Cosgrove.
31 Phyllis Trible observes that although the Greek text states the pilegesh was dead, the Hebrew text is vague, indicating the possibility that the raped woman was still alive when the Levite dismembered her. See Trible, p. 80.
32 Exum, "Raped by the Pen," p. 171.
33 Ibid.
34 Ibid., p. 177
35 Ibid., p. 191.
36 Exum is referencing the pilegesh's act of leaving her husband to return to her father's home. See Judges 19:2.
37 Ibid., pp. 170–201.
38 Tammi J. Schneider, *Judges* (Collegeville: The Liturgical Press, 2000), p. 245.
39 Trible, p. 65.
40 Ibid.
41 Scholz, p. 39.
42 Schroeder, p. 155.
43 See ibid., pp. 153–190 for a detailed history of interpretations of the rape of Tamar.
44 Pamela Tamarkin Reis, "Cupidity and Stupidity: Women's Agency in the 'Rape' of Tamar." *Journal of the Ancient Near Eastern Society* 25 (1998): pp. 43–60, 43.
45 Ibid., p. 50.
46 Ibid.
47 According to this myth, men are not responsible for their actions; instead, males are actually victims of their own uncontainable and instinctive nature.
48 Ken Stone, "Sexual Power and Political Prestige: The Case of the Disputed Concubines." *Bible Review* 10 (1994): pp. 28–31, 52–53. Also see Jon Levenson, "I Samuel 25 as Literature and History." *Catholic Biblical Quarterly* 40 (1978): pp. 11–28; Jon Levenson and Baruch Halpern, "The Political Import of David's Marriages." *Journal of Biblical Literature* 99 (1980): pp. 507–519; Matitihu Tsevat, "Marriage and Monarchical Legitimacy in Ugarit and Israel." *Journal of Semitic Studies* 3 (1958): pp. 237–243.
49 As Stone (p. 30) points out, this custom is not stated in the Hebrew Bible; however, it is a reading hypothesis utilized to interpret literary events.
50 See David M. Gunn, *The Story of King David: Genre and Interpretation*. (Sheffield: Sheffield Academic Press, 1978).
51 Gerhard von Rad, *The Problems of the Hexateuch* (New York: McGraw Hill, 1966), p. 184.
52 Gnana Robinson, *1 & 2 Samuel: Let Us Be Like the Nations* (Grand Rapids: Eerdmans Publishing, 1993), p. 239.
53 Eugene H. Peterson, *First and Second Samuel* (Louisville: Westminster John Knox Press, 1999), p. 215.
54 See A.A. Anderson, *World Biblical Commentary: 2 Samuel*. Vol. 2 (Dallas: World Books, 1989), p. 214; Ernst Wurthwein, *The Text of the Old Testament* (London: SCM Press, 1980).
55 Anderson, p. 214.
56 See Frymer-Kensky.
57 Note that there is no Hebrew word that translates to rape. The word innâ, meaning to overpower, is used in Genesis 34 and the word yadah, meaning to know, is used in Judges 19 and 2 Samuel 13.
58 While the Geneva Convention and its additional protocol of 1977 do prohibit rape, as well as forced prostitution and other forms of sexual assault, these crimes are

categorized as attacks upon personal dignity and honor rather than violent crimes. The Rome Statute of the International Criminal Court, adopted in 1998, pronounces rape and sexual violence war crimes.
59 Stone, p. 31.
60 Schroeder, p. 57.
61 Karen Jo Torjesen, *When Women Were Priests: Women's Leadership in the Early Church and the Scandal of Their Subordination in the Rise of Christianity* (New York: HarperSanFrancisco, 1993), p. 139.
62 Ibid.
63 Livy, Ab *Urbe Condita*, 2:58, quoted in Ian Donaldson, *The Rapes of Lucretia: A Myth and its Transformation* (Oxford: Clarendon, 1982), p. 22.
64 Donaldson, p. 24.
65 Ibid., p. 25.
66 Quoted in ibid., p. 26. See Tertullian, *Ad Martyras*, in Alexander Roberts and James Donaldson (eds) *The Writings of Tertullian*. Whitefish, MT: Kesslinger Publishing, 2011.
67 Commentariorum in Jonam Prophetam Liber Unus (P.L. 25:1129), quoted in Jane Schulenburg, *Forgetful of Their Sex* (Chicago: University of Chicago Press, 1983), p. 34.
68 Jerome, "Epistle 22:5," in *Select Letters of St. Jerome*. Trans. E.A. Wright. LCL 262. Cambridge, MA: Harvard University Press, 1963, quoted in Schroeder, p. 73.
69 Augustine, *The City of God*. Trans. Henry Bettenson, ed. David Knowles (Harmondsworth: Penguin, 1972), bk. i, pp. 29, 30, quoted in Donaldson, p. 29. See ibid., pp. 22–39 for further discussion on Christian interpretations and claims of Lucretia's guilt.
70 Ideas about women's sexuality can be traced back to early discussions of women's role in the Fall and women's association with nature over intellect. See Susan Deacy and Karen Pierce, eds., *Rapes in Antiquity* (London: Duckworth, 1997) for further discussion on the idea of women's sexuality and rape.
71 Suetonius, *The Lives of the Caesars*. ed. J.C. Rolfe (New York: Macmillan, 1924), pp. 380–381.
72 See Schroeder, p. 60. Also see Pseudo-Lucian, *Lucius or The Ass, in Lucian*. Vol. 8. Trans. M.D. MacLeod. LCL 432. Cambridge, MA: Harvard University Press, 1969, pp. 52–145.
73 See Clement, "First Epistle of Clement to the Corinthians 6:2," in *The Apostolic Fathers*. Trans. Kirsopp Lake. LCL 24. Cambridge, MA: Harvard University Press, 1965; Tertullian, *Apology*. CCSL 1:85–171. Turnout: Brepols, 1953. Also see Schroeder, pp. 59–60 for a detailed discussion.
74 Tertullian, *Apology*, CCSL 1:171.
75 Schroeder, p. 62.
76 Ibid.
77 Jan N. Bremmer, *The Apocryphal Acts of Peter: Magic, Miracles and Gnosticism* (Leuven: Peeters, 1998), p. 103.
78 The Acts of Paul and Thecla, 26, in Jan N. Bremmer, *The Apocryphal Acts of Paul and Thecla* (Leuven: Peeters, 1996), p. 50.
79 Ibid.
80 Schroeder, p. 62.
81 Karen A. Winstead, *Virgin Martyrs: Legends of Sainthood in Late Medieval England* (Ithaca: Cornell University Press, 1997), p. 1.
82 Ibid.
83 Pauline Bart and Eileen Geil Moran, *Violence against Women: The Bloody Footprints* (Thousand Oaks, CA: Sage Publications, 1993), p. 108.

84 See Winstead and Maud Burnett McInerney, *Eloquent Virgins: From Thecla to Joan of Arc* (New York: Palgrave Macmillan, 2003) for a more detailed discussion on the historicity of virgin martyrs.
85 Schroeder, p. 58.
86 Winstead, pp. 1–2.
87 Susan Brownmiller, *Against Our Will: Men, Women, and Rape* (New York: Simon & Schuster, 1975), pp. 327–328.
88 See Kathleen Zuanich Young, "The Imperishable Virginity of Saint Maria Goretti," in Carol J. Adams and Marie M. Fortune, eds., *Violence against Women and Children: A Christian Theological Sourcebook* (New York: Continuum, 1995), pp. 279–286. Maria Goretti's canonization in 1950, just forty-eight years after her death, was rushed through with extraordinary speed (at the time of writing, only two other people had been canonized any faster). In addition, she became a model of chastity and her story was part of the curriculum in parochial schools until Vatican II.
89 Pope Pius XII quoted in Young, p. 282.
90 Ibid., p. 279.
91 Brownmiller, p. 331. Note that sources differ as to whether or not Serenelli raped Maria while murdering her, although the Catholic Church's stance is that Maria died a virgin. See Carly Rivers, *Aphrodite at Mid-Century* (Garden City, NY: Doubleday, 1973).
92 Young, p. 284.
93 As previously noted, "the pressure cooker theory of male nature" claims that men are not responsible for their actions and instead are victims of their own uncontainable and instinctive nature. However, rape has very little to do with nature or sexuality. Instead, it is an extremely violent act that is a product of power and control, implemented by sexual means.
94 Young, p. 285.

3 Learning from women's testimony

> I felt like my soul had been crushed. I felt like I wasn't even human anymore. How could anybody love me, or want me, or care about me? I felt like life had no more meaning to it.
>
> Elizabeth Smart[1]

The term "testimony" is used to describe discourse that tells the truth of one's experience. Rather than simply formulating a statement, to testify is a discursive practice that describes events or experiences that cannot be properly described or revealed through rational discourse. It is through women's testimony that buried truths about the harm caused by sexual violence and rape culture can be discovered.

In the previous chapter I discussed the rape of women in religious texts and history along with their interpretations and problematic representations. The ongoing historical and religious legacy of sexual violence against women, rape culture, and spiritual wounding as a result is well documented through their stories. In addition, the voices of the women in these texts have been silenced and their experiences ignored by rape culture. Thus, we must demand that attention be given to the voices and actions of these women and we must learn from their testimony.

While Dinah, the unnamed pilegesh in Judges, and David's ten pilegesh do not speak, their lack of voice must be understood as testimony and evidence of their personal experiences of violence perpetrated not only by their rapists but also by their communities and the male narrators who constructed their stories. Tamar, Lucretia, and Maria Goretti offer testimony that acknowledges their experiences of spiritual wounding as a result of sexual violence. Tamar pleads with Amnon not to rape her; she recognizes that if she is raped great shame will plague her and that she will have no opportunity for a "normal" life. Following the rape, "Tamar put ashes on her head, and tore the long robe that she was wearing; she put her hand on her head, and went away, crying aloud as she went" (2 Samuel 13:19). With these actions, Tamar communicates her deep mourning and experience of spiritual wounding; she also illustrates her recognition that she will be condemned by her community. And Tamar is correct: she is further victimized by the rape culture; she goes to Absalom for help and he orders her to be silent, David takes no action against Amnon for raping his daughter, and we are told that Tamar leads a desolate life because of the shameful fate she suffered at the hands of her brother.

Both Maria Goretti's and Lucretia's willingness to accept death rather than be raped speaks loudly to the suffering they each anticipated as a result of sexual violence. Only after being threatened with the exposure of a false affair following her murder does Lucretia submit to being raped. Her spiritual wounding is so deep that, for her, suicide offers the only possible remedy. For Maria Goretti, submission to sexual violence was not an option and so she accepted death. The silencing of these women, their deep mourning, spiritual suffering, and self-deprecating actions well demonstrate rape culture's historical legacy and manifestation within religion.

Contemporary testimony

According to Elie Wiesel, "If the Greeks invented tragedy, the Romans the epistle, and the Renaissance the sonnet, our generation invented a new literature, that of testimony."[2] Contemporary literature, including that which is written by survivors of sexual violence, utilizes testimony to "describe their discourse, to tell truth as they see it, as they experience it, and what truth means to their communities."[3] Rebecca Chopp explains that, because testimony functions to tell the truth and enact moral consciousness while being sensitive to diverse voices, it is utilized "in order to represent deliberately our communities or movements within the public arena."[4]

In order properly to represent the consequences of rape culture and the physical, emotional, and spiritual wounding resulting from sexual violence, this chapter will present the testimonies of twenty-five women who have suffered such experiences. The testimonies set forth here bridge multiple geographical and cultural boundaries and range from the World War II era to the present. Because sexual violence occurs in different contexts and is perpetrated by persons or groups with varying relationships to the victim, these testimonies will be presented in the following categories: stranger rape; acquaintance rape; marital rape; gang rape; honor rape; rape within war; rape within the military; and trafficking. In the following chapters, these women's testimonies will be referred to in order to elaborate definitions and functions of rape, and rape culture. In addition, these cases will be reflected on thoroughly during discussions of spiritual death and possibilities for spiritual resurrection.

Stranger rape

Although stranger rape is commonly believed to be one of the more prevalent types of rape, its occurrence is rare in comparison to others. Society has wrongfully identified stranger rape as "real rape" – a rape committed by a deranged man who stalks his prey. This understanding is problematic for multiple reasons; however, even with this delusional understanding, women are still subjected to rape culture when sexually victimized by a stranger. The trauma, shame, self-blame, and spiritual wounding endured are not lessened. In the following pages, Susan, Dr. Shazia, Nancy, and Andrea offer testimony about their experiences of stranger rape and describe the impact of their assaults and their suffering following the rapes.

Susan

While walking along a country road one morning, Susan was violently attacked, raped, and left for dead.

> I had been grabbed from behind, pulled into the bushes, beaten and sexually assaulted ... He called me a whore and told me to shut up. Although I had said I'd do whatever he wanted, as the sexual assault began I instinctively fought back, which so enraged my attacker that he strangled me until I lost consciousness. When I awoke, I was being dragged by my feet down into a ravine ... After ordering me to get on my hands and knees ... my assailant strangled me again ... This time I was sure I was dying. But I revived, just in time to see him lunging toward me with a rock. He smashed it into my forehead, knocking me out, and eventually after another strangulation attempt, he left me for dead.
>
> After my assailant left, I managed to climb out of the ravine, and I was rescued by a farmer who called the police, a doctor, and an ambulance. I was taken to emergency ... where I underwent [numerous] tests and a gynecological exam ... I was taken to an office where there were no receptionists and where I was greeted by two male doctors I had never seen before. When they told me to take off my clothes and stand in the middle of the room, I refused. I had to ask for a hospital gown to put on. For about an hour the two of them went over me like a piece of meat, calling out measurements of bruises and other assessments of damage, as if they were performing an autopsy ... I felt as if I was experiencing things posthumously ... I thought, perhaps I did die in that ravine. The line between life and death, once so clear and sustaining, now seemed carelessly drawn and easily erased.

Following her attack, Susan explains that her sense of reality was confused and she feared others would find out that she had been raped.

> I led a spectral existence, not quite sure whether I had died and the world went on without me, or whether I was alive but in a totally alien world ... My sense of unreality was fed by the massive denial of those around me ... I didn't want people to know I had been sexually assaulted. I don't know whether this was because I could still barely believe it myself, because keeping this information confidential was one of the few ways

I could feel in control of my life, or because, in spite of my conviction that I had done nothing wrong, I felt ashamed.[5]

Dr. Shazia

It was a routine day. I left for the hospital and I locked the gate to my residence. At 8pm, I returned and unlocked the gate and then relocked it. I went inside and I ate dinner and said my prayers. I watched a little television and then went to sleep at 10pm. I was sound asleep, and I felt someone pushing my hair. At first, I thought I was dreaming. When he started pushing harder, I woke up. The room was dark. I felt him pushing my neck even harder and I couldn't breathe. I tried to scream. I tried to shout for help. He took a cord, and put it around my neck and began strangling me. I yelled and fought to get away from him, but all my fighting was useless. I was helpless. I tried to reach for the phone that was beside the bed, but he took the receiver and hit me on the head, and then he raped me. I said to him, "For the sake of God, for the sake of Mohammad, I have not wronged you, why are you doing this to me?" He said, "Be quiet." He told me there was a man named Amjad outside with a can of kerosene, and they would set me on fire if I didn't keep quiet. I said to him, "You must have your own sisters, or daughters, or mother." He told me to shut up. He blindfolded me with my scarf, he pistol-whipped me, and he raped me again. When he was done, he covered me with a blanket and tied my wrists with a telephone wire, but he didn't leave. He stayed in my room and watched the English language television. I was badly beaten and I lost consciousness. When I woke up, I was so scared I couldn't breathe. Eventually, I tried to loosen the bindings on my wrist, and I was able to get a hold of scissors to free myself. I then fled to the home of one of the nurses. I was in trauma and shock. I didn't say it, but she could see that I had been raped.

Dr. Shazia was told by her physicians not to tell the police about the rape and they later told the authorities that she did not want to pursue the case. Although she was wounded and bleeding, her injuries were not tended to and she was not allowed to contact her family. Instead, Dr. Shazia was sedated and then sent by charter airplane to a psychiatric hospital in Karachi in secret. Eventually her brother and sister-in-law brought her home and contacted her husband Khalid, who was working in Libya. Dr. Shazia explains:

Khalid immediately called me, and I told him everything that happened. He said he was with me and that I was innocent and that I should go give a statement to the police. He told me not to worry and that it wasn't my fault. On January 9th the police took my statement. We were told by the military intelligence that within 48 hours, the culprit would be caught. We were then moved to another house by the government. We were held there under house arrest. I wanted justice. I know the government knows who the culprit is. A military intelligence officer told us they knew, but they haven't done a thing. In the capital, while we were under house arrest, we saw the President on television. He said that my life was in danger. Meanwhile, Khalid's grandfather declared that I was "kari" [a stain on the family honor] and that Khalid should divorce me and that his family should not have anything more to do with me. I thought I was going to be killed to save the honor of Khalid's family. If I was to be murdered, I thought I should commit suicide. I took a knife, and I went to the bathroom. Khalid sensed what was happening, and he and my adopted son came to stop me. My adopted son said to me, "Mum if you kill yourself, I will also kill myself."[6]

Nancy

While Nancy took her garbage out one evening after dinner, a man crept inside her door and waited for her to return. He then brutally attacked and raped Nancy for hours inside her home.

> I am standing at the sink, washing a pan ... A storm from behind, and impact. It sucks away the air around me in a great rush. I cannot breathe. Rage is turning the air to pumice. I cannot hear. Something in my eyes. The pain is in my eyes. I am closing my eyelids but they do not meet. Something is in my eyes, something is coiling around my neck, something alive. Something furious and terrible. Words, but I cannot hear them. I am thrashing in the air. There is a foul odor. My body is on fire from inside. My blood is rushing as if trying to escape. I hear only it. There is no air. It is all going out of me. Who is screaming? I do not know who is screaming. I cannot breathe.
>   Now I hear the words. These are the words I hear: Shut up shut the fuck up you bitch you dirty bitch you fucking cunt shut up do you hear me you fucking dirty bitch I'm going to kill you if you don't shut up you bitch I am going to kill you.
>   Now I am sucking air into my lungs. I am prey, grasping for air. Now I have a thought: So this is Death. Now I have a feeling: Anything to live. Now I feel something hard pressing against my back. I know what it is. It is a penis.
>   Over the next thee hours he raped me and tormented me with descriptions of how he would kill me.[7]

Following her attacker's exit, Nancy is in shock and cannot remember that 911 is the phone number for an emergency; so instead she dials zero for the operator.

> I held the telephone and pressed the button that had the letters OPER on them and actually wondered if this nightmare was something I had done

to myself ... To say that I had been raped, to use the word, required that I sort out the incubi from the saber tooths from whatever it was that had just destroyed my apartment. I was choking on the word.[8]

After the police arrive, Nancy is questioned by a female officer who tells her that she cannot have any water, stating that she might wash away evidence.

> I want water. My thirst is vicious. I am in the kitchen now. I turn on the faucet at the kitchen sink. My mouth is full of dirt ... Her words were terrible. I want to wash my mouth with fire. What is in my mouth? Dirt is in my mouth. In my body. His dirt.[9]

Nancy is then taken to the hospital by ambulance.

> I hoped for comfort and I sensed that the hospital staff wanted to provide it. But for a rape victim the hospital emergency room functions as an extension of the police department ... After satisfying themselves that I was not seriously injured, the emergency room staff began performing the work of criminologists, collecting evidence that might be used in a court of law. My body was still not my own. It was evidence. I was not a patient whose wounds could be sutured. I was the scene of the crime.[10]
>
> I felt as if being raped were the crime ... The life I saved was not ... my life. I had made a deal with my rapist and now I regretted it. From now on, everyone would assess that deal ... What if he hadn't intended to kill me? Why did I believe his threats? Why didn't I have the physical strength to break his hold in those first few minutes? Was there something about me that allowed me to cave into his demands? Was I a despicable coward? Why had I given in to his hateful needs to spare a life I no longer recognized as my own? ... If I had fought harder I would either be dead or be as I was before. Now I was neither. I was evidence.[11]
>
> In the hospital I felt as I imagined an animal might feel – without words, and therefore without understanding or a sense of sequence ... I wanted "real" wounds then, the kind that bleed. The kind that doctors could stitch up. The kind I imagined the man screaming in the next room had. I had done everything I could to avoid them, but waiting alone, feeling as I did, I realized "real" wounds could be tended. I wanted them. I wondered who it was that was thinking like this because I felt at the same time that I was dying.[12]
>
> The rapist had stolen something at the center of what I had known as myself. It was gone with the cash, credit cards, jewelry, underpants, and whatever else he took. All these things that meant nothing to me might be recovered by the police, but how could this missing self be retrieved? The rapist himself might be caught, but he could never produce the woman who had not been raped.[13]

Andrea

Asleep in bed, Andrea awakes to a man on top of her threatening to hurt her if she makes a sound. As Andrea is brutally raped, she wonders where her daughter and friend are, whether her kitten is still alive, and if she will be cut, shot, or strangled.

> First I think I'm nightmaring ... Then try to sink back under sleep's blanket and weave whatever is going on into a dream ... Then I try to pass out. Can't because I don't know what he'll do, because I am adrenalined 360 degrees opposite of relaxed. Besides, he wants me to be conscious of his omnipotence and my humiliating powerlessness. It's almost blackstrap-molasses dark. And horribly quiet.

During her rape, Andrea focused on survival and getting through her attack.

> I chose life and did what I thought would keep me in the land of the living ... The sustaining, salvific prayers came from friends and ancestors on the other side ... While I moan and whimper, some choir is singing, "I don't know where, but I know that you do. I can't see how, but I know you'll get through. God, please touch somebody right now, right now."
>
> Will he slash my face when he's through? All he asks for is money. Not a demand. A casual request as if I'm "his woman," and he's going to run an errand. Same man who has walked through the walls of my apartment to rape me, waits, almost patiently, while I fumble through two purses for my wallet and he lets me take the bills out. Doesn't count the seventy dollars I hand over or mention my credit cards.

Feeling she must adhere to the "strong-Black-wonder-woman-role" she has been "trained" for, Andrea drives herself to a hospital with which she is completely unfamiliar.

> Since I'm feeling fine (not a single bruise, broken fingernail, or out of place earring), it's a hassle to be in the dry cold of the Clayton Hospital's air-conditioned examining room waiting the hours it takes doctors to finish treating Saturday night knife slashes and bullet gashes before one can get to me. The crisis counselor says I seem like a woman accustomed to being in control and, since rape rendered me powerless, I may have a more difficult recovery than a more passive woman.

Sitting and waiting for treatment, Andrea wonders what stages she will go through before healing. She wonders what other victims' experiences have been but is frustrated that there is little information for her about transcending her rape agony.

> I ask what stages I can expect to go through and what I should do to recover from rape quickly and completely. Suck my teeth and groan to hear "Each victim has to find her own way. It's hard to predict. Women mourn and mend differently ... " Some recovered victim must have chronicled her journey, published her 12-step program, copywritten a recipe I can improve on. Though I scour, I never find a thing.

The medical exam is frightening for Andrea in the aftermath of her rape.

> The counselor describes the hospital's exam and treatment: If there's a chance that I might be pregnant, I'll get the morning-after pill; had the rapist bitten me, I'd get a tetanus shot – BITTEN ME; blood will be drawn to see if I've gotten a sexually transmitted disease, but while waiting for the results, I'm to take antibiotics just in case ... The doctor – a nurse by his side – turns off the light so his ultraviolet lamp can look for traces of rapist's semen between my legs. The second strange man in this long evening standing over my body focused on my vulva. I've neither seen nor heard about this phase of rape's aftermath ... Hairs are pulled, one by one, from my head and vulva for DNA testing. After the lab technicians take my blood and give me a Band-Aid with Daffy Duck decorations, I collapse into snuffling tears, "I was so scared and there was no one to help me."

Following her rape, Anita continually looks for ways to recover but the rape culture continues to assault her.

> My candid talk about being raped surprises because people are accustomed to rape victims' shame and reticence. "But," I say over and over, "I am the victim, not the criminal."[14]
>
> I decide to go into therapy or join a support group. Of the women I know who are rape victims and talk about it ... the one who joined a support group has kept her high-profile job and even traveled to China. Like her I have no intention of letting the rapist mangle my life.[15]
>
> Saying the story I usually claim, "All I asked God for was my life. God gave me that and so much more ... " If you'd told me way back then that I'd still be recovering from rape now ... I wouldn't have believed you. If I'd known, or even suspected, the hells that lurked on the other side of shock, I would have tried to overdose, instead of just asking counselors and psychiatrists how likely it was for rape victims to commit suicide, instead of pleading to be hospitalized until "all this" was over; instead of telling two different, but equally startled psychiatrists, eighteen months and 700 miles apart, to "shoot me and put me out of my misery."[16]

Acquaintance rape

The problem of acquaintance rape is widespread, occurring across the globe, affecting women and girls of all ages. Regardless of culture, ethnicity, religion, social status, income, or other qualifying factors, women and girls are raped by men they know. This being said, "acquaintance rape remains largely hidden because few people identify it for what it is – a crime punishable by law."[17] Sadly, this act of violence against women is often ignored as a crime and instead described in various ways that blame the woman for being loose, or dressed inappropriately, or intoxicated, or not assertive, or for wanting it, and the list goes on. As Robin Warshaw explains, "acquaintance rape is a crime. And it is not less a crime simply because the perpetrator has a familiar face."[18]

The testimonies of Robin, Lori, Rachel, Ruth, and Debbie are detailed below.

Robin

Two months after breaking up with Carl, he went to Robin's apartment and pleaded with her to go with him to a mutual friend's apartment to discuss their relationship, claiming that he was suicidal. Concerned and feeling guilty for making Carl unhappy, Robin agreed. Once they arrived at the apartment, Robin quickly realized it was empty. Carl bolted the door, brandished a large knife, and held her hostage throughout the night.

> When, late into night he motioned to the bedroom with the knife, I followed. In bed, he draped his arm across me, holding the knife on the far side of the pillow all night. He had intercourse with me at least once, but I think it might have been more than that. It seemed to go on for a long time. I felt like I was in a corner of the room, watching the bed from a distance. Eventually, he fell asleep. I did not move. I did not holler. I did not try to leave. In the morning, Carl walked me back to my apartment ... When I finally got inside I stripped off my clothes and stood in the shower for an hour. I did not go to work that day ... I had told no one about the rape.
>
> It took me about three years to realize I had been raped. Before that, all I focused on about the assault was the feeling that I could die. Since my attacker had been my boyfriend with whom I had had sexual intercourse before, I never attached the word "rape" to what happened. Rape, after all, is what vile strangers did to you.
>
> I'd like to say that naming it helped, but it didn't ... The rape contributed to problems I had for the next several years.[19]

Ten years after the rape, Robin received a phone call from Carl on Christmas Eve. Although she was frightened, Robin wanted to confront Carl and asked him if he realized that the last time they had seen each other he had raped her. Carl responded by saying yes, but that the statute of limitations was up.

> I couldn't believe it: I had confronted him and he had admitted that, yes, he had raped me ... By answering "yes" to my question, Carl gave a power to my belief in what happened that it had not had before. I was angry and disappointed in myself that his corroboration could mean so much.[20]

Lori

After agreeing to go on a double date with her friend Amy, Lori joined Eric in the expectation of meeting the other couple at a barbecue. Amy had already told Eric that she and her boyfriend had to cancel, but no one had told Lori of the change of plans. Lori waited, assuming that Amy would arrive; and Eric continually lied, saying that she was coming. Although Lori eventually realized that the double date was not going to happen, she suspected nothing and continued with her date with Eric.

> He grabbed me from behind and picked me up. He had his hands over my eyes and we were walking through his house. It was really dark and I didn't know where on earth he was taking me ... He laid me down and kissed me ... He starts taking off my clothes and I said, "Wait, time out! This is not what I want you know," and he said to me something like this is what I owed him because he made me dinner.
>
> I said, "This is wrong, don't do this. I didn't go out with you with this intent" ... I'm yelling and hitting and pushing on him and he just liked that. He says, "I know you must like this because a lot of women like this kind of thing ... This is the adult world. Maybe you ought to grow up some." I finally got to the point where there was nothing I could do.
>
> He said, "Don't tell me you didn't like that." I looked at him and said, "No," and by this time I'm crying because I don't know what else to do. I never heard of anybody having that happened to them.

Following the rape, Lori felt numb and continually questioned herself, wondering if she had provoked the attack.

> I felt like a zombie. I couldn't cry, I couldn't smile, I couldn't eat ... I thought it was my fault. What did I do to make him think he could do something like that? Was I wrong in kissing him? Was I wrong to go out with him, to go over his house?[21]

Rachel

During her freshman year at a large university, Rachel attended a party in her co-ed dorm. She was talking with a football player who wasn't drinking but was "feeding" her alcohol. He then led her to his room and she was surprised to find there was no one else there.

> I didn't think he'd hurt me. I thought there would be other people there ... When we got to his room and I saw there was nobody there, I didn't think I could do anything about it.
>
> We started kissing and then he started taking off my clothes. I kept telling him to stop and I was crying. I was scared of him and thought he was going to hurt me ... he had a hand over my face. I was five foot two and weighed 110 pounds. I didn't have a choice.
>
> I felt ashamed because it happened. I just felt dirty, violated. I thought it was my fault. It wasn't like he did something to me, it was like I let him do something to me, so I felt very bad about myself.

Rachel's rapist later came to her dorm and asked her to go on a date with him. She refused, but did not report her rape. "Who would believe me? He was a really good football player. No one would have believed me if I said anything. I wouldn't have dreamed of saying anything."[22]

Ruth

As a young college student, Ruth was excited about her position as a research fellow and winning a fellowship to medical school. However, after being raped on a date, she dropped out of school and retired on disability because of the wounding she suffered.

> Going to this guy's apartment and realizing that I was in trouble was disturbing. I really didn't understand what I should have done. I couldn't get out. He had a deadbolt lock, with a key from the inside. He had taken the key out and unplugged the phone. When we drove into the apartment garage, the bars came down. He said, "You should feel secure." I was disoriented. There was no way I could have gotten out of his apartment let alone this building. I was raped for eighteen or nineteen hours. I thought I was going to die.
>
> He told me while he was raping me about the therapy group he was in. He told me he had a criminal record, and he'd done this dozens of times before. He was older, thirty-two. Hated his mother and the Catholic Church. Hated virgins. I was a virgin. I just remember thinking about what I could hit him with. Every time I moved, he moved – all night. It was horrible.
>
> The next day, after the rapes, he just dropped me off at the family where I was staying, and I just told myself, "Oh well, nothing happened ... " I just hypnotized myself and forgot the whole thing. Just shut down ... Didn't think about it at all until about nine years later. In my mind I castrated him. I have fantasized him being on a jail ward and in

restraints and I would castrate him. And then he would go to prison forever until he died.

When the post trauma of the rape hit, I was partway through medical school. I ended up dropping out. I wanted to be a surgeon. It's too late for me now. I really feel that way. I'm so gone in terms of my concentration and the damage that was done was so huge. I know I can't get back what I lost.

Ruth explains that she often tells people she was date raped to create distance between herself and them.

> Because people don't want to hear it. You can talk about being mugged and boast about being held up at knife point on Market Street Bridge or something, but you can't talk about being raped. And I know if I do, I can't count on that person ever being a friend again … They always treat me different. People have one or two reactions when they see you being needy. They either … exploit you or … they abandon you.[23]
>
> I just decided I wasn't going to date. I don't have sex. I don't have the equipment to deal with it, to keep myself safe. So every man is a rapist and a batterer until proven otherwise. I have anger around not being taught what every young girl should be taught about how to protect herself.
>
> My mother will say now, "So and so was raped." And I'll say, "Well I was too, Mother." Then I get this dead silence. She still hasn't even said, "I'm sorry," or "That's too bad." She hasn't said a word about me being raped. We haven't been together for years. She's still in very strong denial about my rape, which I now pretty much accept.[24]

Ruth explains that she believes race also impacts her experience as a victim.

> One of my frustrations is knowing we black women accept being raped. And middle-class black women don't talk about rape. We sort of support society in viewing us not being important as rape victims. Or we pretend it doesn't really happen. "She's just saying it." Or, "You could have gotten out if you wanted to." Maybe it's a defense; we don't have control over our own sexuality historically – ever – with rape during slavery and all that.[25]

Debbie

After several months of living with and dating Jim, Debbie was fed up with his drug use and abuse and decided to end the relationship. However, Jim refused to accept Debbie's decision and began to harass and repeatedly abuse and rape her.

> He got into my bed and repeatedly tried to rip my underwear off. I kept screaming no and ran into the bathroom. He was right behind me.

> He slammed me into a counter and attempted to choke me and punch me in the head ... I thought of running down the hall out my door, but he had me trapped ... He then threw me from the doorway of the bedroom onto the bed. I was scared to death! He tore my clothes off and tried to enter me vaginally but couldn't do it. I was too dry. Then he tried anally. I thought, "He's hurting me, and now he wants to have sex with me."
>
> For hours, it seemed, he slammed my uterus with what felt like a baseball bat. I lay there, not looking at him, not fighting, passive. He had my ankles held back over my head. All the time he kept saying, "I'm punishing you because you've been a bad girl. I'm giving it to you for every time you've screwed someone."
>
> The punishment lasted for five hours ... I felt like he was ripping me from inside out. I had ripping, searing pain – the most severe pain I've ever felt. I was sobbing uncontrollably.

Later that night, Jim attacked Debbie again. Although she called 911 and reported the rapes, he was not charged. Jim continued to harass Debbie and, finally, he was arrested and charged with sexual assault. During sentencing, although Jim confessed to rape, Debbie's character was repeatedly challenged and she was blamed for her victimization.

> The defense attorney said, "She just picks up on men, and when she gets tired of them, she just throws them away." Much of the talk at sentencing involved my moral character – after he had already confessed ... I felt that a lot of people thought I was dirty, that I'd been to bed with him before, and therefore, I'd take him back. It was like I had no right to press charges.[26]

Marital rape

Rape laws were originally enacted to protect the property of men rather than to protect a woman's right to safeguard and control her own body. Marital rape, also known as spousal or wife rape, was first made illegal in the United States only in 1975, and it remains legal in thirteen countries.[27] According to Raquel Bergen, society's perception of marital rape downplays the seriousness of this violent act. "Within the larger society, wife rape is often understood as a relatively innocuous incident in which a husband wants to have sex, his wife rejects him, and he holds her down on the bed and has intercourse with her ... this scenario is far from the norm."[28] While this scenario should certainly be understood as rape, experiences of marital rape are wide ranging and involve different levels of physical force, frequency, and duration, as with any form of sexual violence.

The testimonies of Kayla, Sally, Karen, and Debbie are detailed below.

Kayla

Rape was a common occurrence in Kayla's marriage. After being raped, Kayla would clean herself, justify the assault, and try to forget that it had occurred in order to cope. She lived in the "eggshell" phase of the cycle of violence and was constantly careful not to anger her husband, recognizing that the violence could escalate at any time.

> He gave me that wild look. You know, that sick look. And I thought, "Oh no, I don't want to do this." But I just knew there was no way to pass it off or get away ... I didn't want to, but I felt pinned down and forced by his weight on top of me. I just wanted to get it over with ... I thought I had to ... I would lay there and pretend it's not happening to me. I would think of shopping or the kids or whatever else I had to do. He fell asleep and I got up and cleaned myself up and then pretended that nothing happened. I thought about the kids coming over, and I just didn't deal with it. I thought to myself, it wasn't that bad.[29]

Kayla explains that, because she was married, she believed she was obligated to have sex with her husband and had no right to refuse him. "Nobody ever told me I had the right to say no. I knew it was yucky and I dreaded it, but I thought I had to do it."[30]

Sally

Sally experienced rape multiple times throughout her marriage. She explains that her husband believed that he was entitled to sex and he often punished Sally by raping her when he felt he was wronged in some way by her or others.

> I think he thought that I was his wife, and he could do anything to me ... He had been physical for a while, and he just worked [the rape] right in, just one night he worked it in. There was no warning and no building its way up ... I remember thinking it's the same thing as a woman being raped. I remember crying and not being able to leave the bed, and in my head, I knew what I was going through was rape.[31]

Sally describes recognizing the constant risk of being sexually assaulted.

> You know what's going to happen, and you're trying to think in your brain, how can I stop this without getting hurt? And you don't know how to stop it without angering him because you know you're going to get killed, and it's like looking a murderer straight in the eye, and they have this cold-blooded look, and you know you're dead unless you can do something.[32]

Like Kayla, Sally also felt she needed to clean herself following her experiences of being raped and she explains that she felt like a rape victim.

> I went into the shower and I washed myself and scrubbed myself. I did everything a rape victim would do. Everything. It was like you knew what had been done to you and that this was something all rape victims do. And you knew you had to heal yourself because if you didn't heal yourself, nobody else would.[33]

When Sally went to the police, the officers were not supportive and did not take her complaints seriously. Instead, she felt mocked and embarrassed.

> The police wouldn't come out, and when they did, they didn't even take the knife and they didn't want me to press charges. I wanted to have a rape kit done and asked for a woman, and they said there was no woman. There was no one to speak to me.
>
> I had to go to the state police, and then I had to go through three detectives and explain everything and be totally embarrassed, and I had to talk about penises and how he ejaculated and how he did certain things. I had to do it with the recorder on, and they kept saying, "Could you say that again miss, speak up, miss, and call it this and that, miss." And "What kind of underwear were you wearing miss? Were you wearing fancy negligees?"[34]

Karen

Karen was involved in an abusive marriage, and rape became a normal part of the violence that she suffered. After the first rape, Karen decided that she must leave and began to save and prepare for an escape. Within the two months that it took her to save and develop a plan, she was raped eleven more times.

> So he beat me up for a half hour, I guess, and then he said, "OK, bitch, get back upstairs," and I knew he wanted sex just by the way he said it. I said, "I can't do that now because I'm really upset and I can't make love to someone who just beat me up" ... and he said "now," and he turned off the stove and ripped off my pajamas and started punching me ... and I got into the corner and was all curled up and he picked me up and threw me on the bed and did his thing. It was disgusting, and afterward I got up and threw up.[35]

Karen explains that she immediately recognized her rape as real and comparable to the experience of a stranger rape. For Karen, the fear of being raped far outweighed her fear of physical violence.

> It was very clear to me. He raped me. He ripped off my pajamas, he beat me up ... it wasn't any different because I was married to him, it

was rape – real clear what it was ... you're at home with your husband, and you don't expect that. I was under constant terror even if he didn't do it.[36]

Karen states that the rape was not just one more aspect of being battered; she says it was much more than that and far worse than the physical violence. Although she was encouraged by her priest to return to the abusive relationship, she states that she could no longer subject herself to the abuse, particularly the rape.[37]

Debbie

Debbie was in a very abusive marriage and was raped as many as three times a day for eight years. She explains that often when her husband was drinking he would rape her until he passed out from exhaustion. According to Debbie, she often lay quietly while her husband raped her with various objects for fear that if she struggled, she would suffer internal injuries. "To say he was very rough was an understatement. He beat me until I was bruised and bleeding and then used anything – like a hairbrush, broken beer bottles, or anything – to put inside me."[38]

Debbie explains that she would "orb out" and mentally leave her body in order to cope with the constant terror and brutal rapes. Because her experiences of rape took place within marriage, she felt it was impossible to reach out for help.[39]

Gang rape

Gang rape is defined as a rape that is perpetrated by two or more assailants. According to Brownmiller, "When men rape in pairs or gangs, the sheer physical advantage of their position is clear-cut and unquestionable. No simple conquest of man over woman, group rape is the conquest of men over Woman."[40] Men experience a bonding with one another when participating in a gang rape and also earn status within their group by proving their sexual abilities. The group leader is given the "honor" of being the first to rape the woman and then the others follow in order of status. Gang rape occurs in a multitude of circumstances, including fraternities, the military, war, and other situations where men are grouped together and challenged to prove their masculinity. The goal is to "humiliate the victim beyond the act of rape through the process of anonymous mass assault."[41]

The testimonies of Amy and "Qatif Girl" are presented below.

Amy

Amy was attending a fraternity party where she consented to having intercourse with Tim, a man she had been dating and with whom she had had intercourse in the past. After using the restroom and returning to the room she was surprised to find a second man undressed and in the bed. According to Amy, she had consented to "threesomes" in the past and thought perhaps that Tim had invited the man into the bed; thus, Amy was passive as the man started to kiss her. However, Tim then exited the room and Amy quickly wanted to end the sexual encounter. She repeatedly asked where Tim was going; however, she was told not to worry about where he was and that she would figure out what was happening soon.

> The door opened and some other guys came in. I think maybe two or three came in at that point. Then, I don't know how, but I went from sitting on the edge of the bed to lying down without the towel wrapped around me ... and this guy was on top of me, and there was intercourse going on. Then the other guys in the room would either come over and one would be like touching me while another was having intercourse or whatever. There was somebody leaning on me most of the time, which made me feel like I was being held down. One person sat on the bed and the other person would sit on my chest with their penis in my mouth or something. It was not like they were saying "You can't leave," but I felt like that's what they were saying.
>
> At various times, I said "That hurts, please stop doing it, please leave me alone." All I heard them say was "That doesn't hurt, you like that. You don't want to leave now." At one point there was some anal penetration, which was really painful. I was crying and somebody held my hand ... After the first twenty minutes or so I passed out and didn't wake up until about six in the morning ... for two hours the guys must have been coming in and out. When I woke up there was some guy sitting on my chest with his knees on both sides of my head. I told him to get the hell off me ... and he said, "What are you doing? I haven't come yet."

Amy pushed the man off and saw there was a second man in the room. She had no clothes on and was confused about what was happening. The two men left the room and Amy got dressed and headed home. She states that she must have passed out and it was two hours before she regained consciousness. During that time men were coming in and out of the room, taking turns raping her. She did not know how many men sexually assaulted her that evening.

> I felt terrible ... my eyes were puffy and swollen, and my face was puffed ... My lips were bleeding and my jaws were stiff. I couldn't smile. My mouth hurt and my lips felt raw. My anus and vagina also felt sore ... I knew I had been the victim of a gang bang ... I felt real stupid about being in such a vulnerable position. I was very angry at myself for getting drunk. This made me feel that I was somewhat responsible, but I felt that they were also responsible.[42]

"Qatif Girl"

The anonymous woman who has become known internationally as "Qatif Girl" was brutally gang-raped by seven men. After feeling threatened by a man she had a relationship with over the phone, she agreed to meet with him in order to retrieve a photo of her that she had given him. While she was with the man, they were both kidnapped, taken to a deserted location, and "Qatif Girl" was repeatedly raped and beaten.

> He started to drive me home ... We were 15 minutes from my house. I told him that I was afraid and that he should speed up. We were about to turn the corner to my house when they [another car] stopped right in front of our car. Two people got out of their car and stood on either side of our car. The man on my side had a knife. They tried to open our door. I told the individual with me not to open the door, but he did. He let them come in. I screamed.
>
> One of the men brought a knife to my throat. They told me not to speak. They pushed us to the back of the car and started driving. We drove a lot, but I didn't see anything since my head was forced down.

The men took "Qatif Girl" to an isolated area where they forced her out of the car and repeatedly raped her.

> They forced me out of the car. They pushed me really hard ... took me to a dark place. Then two men came in. They said, "What are you going to do? Take off your abaya." They forced my clothes off. The first man with the knife raped me. I was destroyed. If I tried to escape, I don't even know where I would go. I tried to force them off but I couldn't. [Another] man ... came in and did the same thing to me. I didn't even feel anything after that.
>
> I spent two hours begging them to take me home. I told them that it was late and that my family would be asking about me. Then I saw a third man come into the room. There was a lot of violence. After the third man came in, a fourth came. He slapped me and tried to choke me.
>
> The fifth and sixth ones were the most abusive. After the seventh one, I couldn't feel my body anymore. I didn't know what to do. Then a very fat man came on top of me and I could no longer breathe.
>
> Then all seven came back and raped me again. Then they took me home ... When I got out of the car, I couldn't even walk. I rang the doorbell and my mother opened the door. She said "you look tired." I didn't eat for one week after that, just water. I didn't tell anyone. I went to the hospital the next day.
>
> The criminals started talking about it [the rape] in my neighborhood. They thought my husband would divorce me. They wanted to ruin my reputation. Slowly my husband started to know what had happened.

> Four months later, we started a case. My family heard about the case. My brother hit me and tried to kill me.

While the seven men were prosecuted for the gang rape, shockingly "Qatif Girl" was also sentenced to 200 lashes for being in a car with a man who was not a relative. While Saudi Arabia's Ministry of Justice defended the sentence, international outrage led to the woman being pardoned by King Abdullah. Following the rape and international attention on her case, "Qatif Girl" states that she has been humiliated and devastated and wants to die. "Everyone looks at me as if I'm wrong. I couldn't even continue my studies. I wanted to die. I tried to commit suicide twice."[43]

Honor rape

Honor rape is a form of gang rape and a manifestation of rape culture found primarily in some Islamic societies. Its function is to punish and shame a family for its misdeeds. Honor, or izzat, is connected to the sense of the man's right to possess and control women. Men possess honor by objectifying honor in the person of a woman. Conversely, women cannot possess honor in the same way that men can; instead, they symbolize honor. Because of this objectification, the community does not recognize women as individuals.

> Raping a woman robs a man of his most prized possession, his honor, but it obliterates a woman's whole being. Once a man's honor is violated, all he can do, all he is expected to do, all he should do is to seek revenge. As for the raped woman, no one cares – or dares to care; she doesn't exist as an individual.[44]

As Khalid Ahmed explains,

> Feuds are settled through rapes. Men avenge themselves on each other by raping each other's mothers, wives, daughters and sisters. A brave adversary is supposed to break down under the grief and dishonor of the violation of his womenfolk. At times, women are gang raped, then paraded naked in the streets to show to the society that terminal revenge has been taken.[45]

In addition to functioning as a tool of punishment and shaming for men, honor rape is utilized to punish women for committing acts that the community views as shaming. For instance, in 2006 a mother and daughter were abducted and gang-raped for twelve days because the daughter had continued her education and earned a master's degree. She had done so against the wishes of her village and was charged with defiling her community.

In 2002 such a crime was committed against Mukhtar Mai. She was sentenced by a tribal council to gang-rape by four men for her adolescent brother's crime of allegedly having an affair with a woman in a tribe of higher prestige. Mukhtar was taken into a room and gang-raped at gunpoint in front of 200 witnesses. The following is her testimony.

Mukhtar

> Abdul Khaliq turns to his kinsmen, who are as eager as he is to carry out that verdict, to demonstrate their power through a show of force. Abdul Khaliq then grabs my arm, while Ghulam Farid, Alla Dita, and Mohammed Faiz start pushing me.
>
> I am there, true, but it isn't me anymore: this petrified body, these collapsing legs no longer belong to me. I am about to faint, to fall to the ground, but I never get the chance – they drag me away like a goat led to slaughter. Men's arms have seized mine, pulling at my clothes, my shawl, my hair. "In the name of the Koran, release me!" I scream. "In the name of God, let me go!"

Mukhtar is repeatedly raped while an armed man stands guard at the door.

> Escape is impossible. Prayer is impossible. That is where they rape me, on the beaten earth of an empty stable ... I don't know how long that vicious torture lasts. An hour? All night?
>
> I ... lose all consciousness of myself, but I will never forget the faces of those animals. For them, a woman is simply an object of possession, honor, or revenge. They marry or rape them according to their conception of tribal pride. They know that a woman humiliated in that way has no other recourse except suicide. They don't even need to use their weapons. Rape kills her. Rape is the ultimate weapon: it shames the other clan forever.
>
> Then they shove me outside, half naked, where I stumble and fall. They throw my shalwar at me ... Everyone is waiting. I am alone with my shame before the eyes of the entire village. I have no words to describe what I am at that moment. I can't think: a dense fog has clouded my brain, masking the images of torture and infamous submission.
>
> My mother is weeping outside our home. I walk past her, dazed, mute, accompanied in silence by other women. I enter one of the three rooms in the women's quarters and crumple onto a straw pallet, where I lie motionless under a blanket. My life has just collapsed into such horror that my mind and body will not accept reality ... For three days, I leave that room only to relieve myself, but I never eat, or cry, or speak.[46]
>
> I have made up my mind: I want to kill myself. That is what women in my situation do. I will swallow acid and die, to put out forever the fire of shame that torments my family and me. I beg my mother to help me die. She must go buy some acid so that my life may finally end, since I'm already dead in the eyes of others![47]

Mukhtar explains that her mother convinces her not to commit suicide and promises to help her recover.

> At twenty-eight years old ... imprisoned by shame in this room, God is my only comfort in my loneliness. Death? Or revenge? How can I recover my honor?
>
> I feel guilty for having been raped, and that is a cruel feeling, because what happened a few days ago was not my fault ... But I cannot forget, and I cannot speak to anyone about what happened to me – it's just not done. Besides, talking about the rape would be unbearable for me, and whenever fresh memories of that appalling night invade my thoughts, I drive them frantically from my mind. I don't want to remember! But I can't help it.[48]

Rape within war

According to Ruth Seifert, rapes are part of the rules of war.[49] Looking back into history, there is a common practice of violence against women in a conquered territory and women are conceded to the victor following the war. Raping women was, and is, a symbolic demonstration of dishonoring the men of the community. In addition, rape is utilized to terrorize communities, physically displace them, and commit genocide. Nations and groups are physically destroyed by rape. "Breaking down the women is a very effective method for breaking down the community."[50]

In modern times, rape has become refined as a military tactic with the purpose of destroying entire communities and nations. As warfare has changed and evolved, women have become objects of strategic importance, and have been utilized to demonstrate how destructive armed forces can be. Within war, women have been forced into roles as "toilets," as the Japanese soldiers referred to comfort women, as well as surrogates for men's honor, unwilling child-bearers, and the list continues. The sexual objectification of women combined with the extraordinary power of the military during war increase the ways to enact violence against women.

The testimonies of B., Jan, I., and Honorata are detailed below.

B.

B. is a Muslim woman from Doboj who was taken prisoner by Serbian troops during the wars in the former Yugoslavia. She recounts how she was repeatedly raped while in custody and recognized some of the men who were sexually assaulting her and the other women and girls being held with her.

> It began as soon as I arrived. They told us not to look at the soldiers so that we wouldn't remember them. We were not allowed to talk with each other. During the day, we stayed in a big sports hall. The guards were

> always there. If they caught us talking, they would take a woman out, beat her and more than the usual [number of men] would rape her. They liked to punish us. They would ask women if they had male relatives in the city; I saw this one woman, and they brought her fourteen year old son and forced him to rape her.
>
> Some of us were selected by name; some would just get chosen. If a man could not rape [i.e., if he was physically unable] he would use a bottle or gun or he would urinate on me.

According to B., local Serbs, including doctors she had worked with and knew personally, raped her and other women who were being held prisoner. Although they attempted to hide their identities, B. immediately recognized them.

> Some of the local Serbs wore black stockings on their heads to disguise their faces because they didn't want to be recognized. [Nevertheless,] I recognized many of them. [They were] colleagues – doctors with whom I worked. The first [man] who raped me was a Serbian doctor named Jodic. I had known Jodic for ten years. We worked in the same hospital. I would see him every day in the employees' cafeteria. We spoke generally, "Hi how are you." He was a very polite, nice man. Another doctor whom I had previously known also raped me; [his name was] Obrad Filipovic. I wasn't allowed to say anything. Before he raped me he said, "Now you know who we are. You will remember forever." I was so surprised; he was a doctor!
>
> Once I saw the face of a woman I knew; her daughter was with her. Three men were with them inside [the classroom]. I was brought in by one man, and another four men followed. On that occasion, I was raped with a gun by one of the three men already in the room. I didn't recognize him. Others stood watching. Some spat on us. They were raping me, the mother and her daughter at the same time. Sometimes you had to accept ten men, sometimes three. Sometimes when they were away, they wouldn't call me for one or two days. I wanted nothing, not bread, not water, just to be alone. I felt I wanted to die. We had no change of clothes and couldn't wash ourselves.[51]

Jan

Jan was held captive in a Japanese prisoner-of-war camp at Ambarawa during World War II. Eventually she was selected and forcibly sent to a house where she became a "comfort woman." Below, she describes the horrifying details of that night.

> Because we were virgins, prices were high on opening night. As soon as it began to get dark, we huddled together in the dining room around the table, terrified ... Never before had I felt such paralysing fear, or felt so helplessly

trapped. We sat there waiting, shaking, crying, holding each other close. By now, the fear had completely overpowered my body. Even to this day I shall never forget it, and in a way it has been there with me, all of my life.

One by one, the girls were taken, crying, protesting, screaming, kicking and fighting with all their might. This continued until all the girls were forcibly taken to their rooms.

Jan's heart pounded as she listened to the cries of the other girls while hiding under the dining-room table. However, it was only a matter of time before she was found.

> Sitting crouched up under the table, I saw the boots almost touching me. Then I was dragged out. A large, repulsive, fat, bald-headed [Japanese man] stood in front of me, looking down at me, grinning at me. I kicked him on the shin. He just stood there, laughing ... [He] stood there, looking down at me. He was in total control of the situation. He had paid a lot of money for opening night and he was obviously annoyed and becoming angry ... Taking his sword out of the scabbard, he pointed it at me, threatening me with it, yelling at me ... "I'll kill, I'll kill!" he shouted.
>
> At that moment I really wanted to die. Dying was better than giving in to this man and being raped by him ... I told [him] that he could kill me, that I was not afraid to die and that I would not give myself to him ...
>
> He threw me on the bed and tore at my clothes, ripping them off. I lay there naked on the bed as he ran his sword slowly up and down, over my body. I could feel the cold steel touching my skin as he moved the sword across my throat and breasts, over my stomach and legs ...
>
> I can find no words to describe this most inhumane and brutal rape. To me, it was worse than dying. My whole body was shaking. I was in a state of shock. I felt cold and numb ...
>
> As soon as he had gone, I gathered what was left of my clothing and ran to the bathroom, feeling that if only I could wash everything away from my body it would be all right. In the bathroom, I found the other girls all crying all trying to do the same thing. Trying to wash away all that had happened to us ... I left the bathroom and hid in a room on the back verandah. My heart was pounding furiously in my body. My whole body was shaking with fear ...
>
> After a while, the angry voices and the sound of heavy army boots came closer and I was dragged out of my hiding place. The night was only young; it was not yet over. There were more Japanese waiting. The terror started all over again ... This was only the beginning ... I had never realised that suffering could be this intense.[52]

Jan had wanted to be a Catholic nun before entering the prison camp; and after her imprisonment came to an end she still wished to follow that dream and dedicate her life to the Church. When she finally met with a priest and shared her story, Jan was told that she could not become a nun because of her experience as a "comfort woman."

> Looking back I realise that the advice he [the priest] gave me was totally wrong and unnecessarily cruel. I was shattered and sadly disappointed by what I had been told. It gave me a terrible inferiority complex. Was I not good enough now to embrace the religious life? Had I suddenly changed? Was I soiled and dirty?
>
> I came for understanding and support and instead walked away totally confused, neglected, unwanted and unloved. I had always regarded the words of a priest as absolute, so I did not question his opinion.[53]

Jan explains that the silence around the violence committed against her was agonizing. "Fifty years of nightmares, of sleepless nights. Fifty years of pain that could never go away, horrific memories embedded in the mind, always there to be triggered off."[54]

I.

I. is a young woman who was captured by rebels in Sierra Leone during its civil war. Each day she was used as a human shield by her captors and watched as other young girls were killed; in the evenings she was repeatedly gang-raped.

> It was late afternoon. I was washing dishes at the river with six other girls. We tried to run, but they caught us. Three girls resisted. To punish them, the rebels cut off their ears. They knifed out their eyes. Then they killed them. I was so afraid, I couldn't move. They said if we struggled, they would kill us too. They raped us. They held me down. It was the first time I had sex.
>
> Each night we were tied by the ankles to the girl next to us. The rebels had sex with us in the presence of everyone. It was always different men. Every time, they hurt me. If I cried, they beat me. I prayed all the time I would not become pregnant.

During the month that I. was held prisoner she was forced to work and was often beaten. Her shoes were taken and she was forced to walk barefoot up to forty kilometers a day carrying heavy loads. She was constantly told that she deserved to be punished. I. states that because of the rapes she endured she feels ashamed and believes she will now not be able to marry. "A Muslim man wants a virgin wife. No one will want me. It's very shameful."[55]

Honorata

Honorata was captured in eastern Congo and held prisoner for eighteen months, during which she was repeatedly and brutally raped.

> I was everybody's woman and nobody's woman. Whoever wanted to satisfy his sexual needs came on us. Sometimes they would shout, "Food! Food!" We thought maybe they were bringing us food. But unfortunately, it was not food. It was us, the women, who were their "food."
>
> Sometimes, when they said that you were the most beautiful woman, it was a disaster! They put you in the middle of everyone, on a cross, with your head down and your legs spread and they raped you in that position. And the others had to cheer them on and dance around you.

Although Honorata was able to escape her captors, after walking 350 kilometers, she found herself in the midst of the Mutebutsi rebellion of 2004 and was raped again.

> When these people raped us, I remember I bled for more than two weeks. I had five different sexually transmitted diseases. I was in Panzi Hospital for over two months.
>
> I know that for the women in rural areas rape is still happening. The war is still there. We are dealing with the effects but not the causes. The cause is all those rapists scattered in the forests. When they bump into a woman, they rape her. They find a woman in a field, they rape her. The woman will sow but she will never be able to harvest. She wants to go to draw water, but instead of water she will find the rapists there, they will rape her and leave her. Sometimes, they will rape her and then kill her.

Honorata now lives with her children. She has not seen her husband since she was kidnapped and believes he would reject her because of her rape.

> I could never imagine such things happening to me in life. I knew I had nearly finished my life, that I had my husband, my children and my work. I had planned everything and now I was really lost. When I came here to Bukavu, I didn't want to see anyone. I avoided people, I shut myself away and it was terrible. If now I can talk, it's because I saw that if everybody keeps silent, the world will never know what's happening here. Really the women are suffering.[56]

Rape within the military

Rape in the military is a serious problem that demands attention. According to Representative Jane Harman in 2010, "a female soldier in Iraq is more likely to be raped by a fellow soldier than killed by enemy fire."[57] Termed "military sexual trauma" by government organizations, sexual violence – including sexual harassment, sexual assault, and rape – is a well-known, ongoing issue within the armed forces. The House Committee on Veterans' Affairs conducted a study that found that 60 percent of women in the National Guard and Reserves have been victims of "military sexual trauma."[58]

Although a high percentage of women are experiencing sexual violence in the military, there has been very little response to this issue. Jane Harman explains:

> According to the DOD statistics, only 181 out of 2,212 subjects investigated for sexual assault in 2007 ... were referred to courts-martial [8 percent of rapes reported] ... Another 218 were handled via nonpunitive administrative action or discharge, and 201 subjects were disciplined through "nonjudicial punishment," which means they may have been confined to quarters, assigned extra duty or received a similar slap on the wrist. In nearly half of the cases investigated, the chain of command took no action; more than a third of the time, that was because of "insufficient evidence."[59]

In 2012, although there were nearly 4,000 reports of sexual assault in the military, only 191 defendants were prosecuted.[60] Women are experiencing high rates of sexual violence; accountability is lacking for those who commit such acts; and the military itself is pervaded by rape culture. Thus, there is little opportunity for healing; and women who are raped also suffer deep psychosocial and spiritual wounding.

The testimonies of Rebekah, Katie, and Angela are presented below.

Rebekah

A former army sergeant, Rebekah was deployed to Afghanistan from 2006 to 2007. She explains that her stress level was the result of more than her deployment – she was continually sexually harassed and abused by a team leader. Although she had survived her year overseas in the war, one week before she was due to return home, she was raped by a superior officer. Devastated by the rape, Rebekah decided not to report it for fear of retaliation.

> One week before my unit was scheduled to return back to the United States, I was raped by another service member that had worked with our team. Initially, I chose not to do a report of any kind because I had no faith in my chain of command as my first sergeant previously had sexual harassment accusations against him and the unit climate was extremely sexist and hostile in nature towards women. After disclosing my rape to a few close friends, I ended up filing a restricted report sixty days before

> I left active duty against both my rapist and my team leader, but had no intentions of ever doing a formal investigation.

Rebekah returned to the US and attempted to begin a new life. She struggled with post-traumatic stress and depression and a year after leaving active duty she was retraumatized when she encountered her rapist.

> Approximately a year after separating from active duty, I was on orders for job training and during that time I ran into my rapist in a post store. He recognized me and told me that he was stationed on the same installation. I was so re-traumatized from the unexpectedness of seeing him that I removed myself from training and immediately sought out assistance from an Army chaplain who told me, among other things, that the rape was God's will and that God was trying to get my attention so that I would go back to church. Again, I did not file an unrestricted report against my rapist.
>
> Six months later, a friend called me and told me they had found pictures of me online that my perpetrator had taken during my rape. At that point, I felt that my rape was always going to haunt me unless I did something about it so I went to Army Criminal Investigation Division (CID) and a full investigation was completed. The initial CID interview was the most humiliating thing that I have ever experienced. I had to relive the entire event for over four hours with a male CID agent whom I had never met and explain to him repeatedly exactly what was happening in each one of the pictures that were found. After the interview was completed, I heard nothing from the investigator until four months later when CID requested that I come back in to repeat my statement to a new investigator who was taking over my case. I almost refused. During the four months of waiting ... I lived in constant fear that I might run into my rapist again or that he might retaliate against me in some way. I decided to continue with the case ... six months later, I was told that even though my rapist had admitted to having "consensual" sex with me while married, his chain of command refused to pursue any charges of adultery and the case was closed.

According to Rebekah, her case is little different from others – evidence that the criminal justice system within the military is broken.

> I feared retaliation before and after I reported, the investigative process severely re-traumatized me, many of the institutional systems set up to help failed me miserably, my perpetrator went unpunished despite admitting to a crime against the Uniform Code of Military Justice (UCMJ), and commanders were never held accountable for making the choice to do nothing.[61]

Katie

Katie, a private in the US military, was ordered by her sergeant to clean a restroom. She entered the restroom and quickly realized it was not in use. Her sergeant walked in behind her and ordered her to lock the door. Katie instantly recognized she was in danger and became sick to her stomach. Fearing what would happen if she did not obey, she complied with the sergeant and locked the door. He ordered Katie to unbutton her pants and promised to pass her on her project for the day.

> I begged him not to do this to me and wouldn't undo my pants. He got aggressive and shoved me against the wall and ripped my pants open. All the time he kept saying, "Don't scream or make a noise because who do you think they'll believe – a private or an experienced sergeant?"
>
> Then he started sticking his tongue in and out and tried to French-kiss me. I held my teeth closed tight. He started talking dirty to me and said he knew I wanted his cock so bad, deep inside of me, and that he could give it to me better than anyone. He kept holding his dick and wanted me to suck on it, but I kept turning my head and closing my teeth tight. He backed me up against a wall and held my neck with his hands and shoved his cock between my legs.

The sergeant threatened Katie after the rape, stating if she reported it he would claim she was crying rape. Deeply traumatized by the attack, Katie felt she needed to tell someone, so she confided in her female squad leader. The squad leader reported the rape, but Katie quickly felt that she was under attack rather than offered assistance by the military police. Terrified, she decided to lie about who her rapist was in order to protect herself from his threats.

According to Katie, the military quickly employed various tactics to cover up the rape. Although she had originally lied about who the rapist was, Katie eventually told the truth, but she was not believed and she felt blamed for the incident both by the military and by her own mother.

> I was sent home for two weeks and when I told my mom the truth, she was furious and yelled at me ... She was mad that I had lied, and she was angry about the rape itself. She didn't really believe it was a traumatic assault, and I felt more ashamed than ever ... my mom blamed me for what had happened.

After returning to the base, Katie felt she was being punished for the rape. She was not allowed to return to school and was continually assigned to unpleasant jobs usually reserved for those who were being disciplined. Eventually, the case was closed without any input from Katie and she was not notified about it. In addition, although there was evidence against the sergeant and he was discharged from the military, no legal action of any kind was brought against him. After the case was closed and Katie was sent to another base, the rape continued to haunt her.

> I was relieved to be sent to another base and to start school again. I felt that I would have a fresh start with no rumors. I was wrong again. You see, your military records follow you everywhere.
> If I had it all to do over again, I probably wouldn't tell. The punishment, shame, and humiliation I felt in the months afterward were worse than the rape itself.[62]

Angela

After experiencing a rape in the military, Angela explains that she felt more victimized by the military itself than by the man who sexually assaulted her.

> You know for me it is not my rapist [by] which I feel the most violated, but by the military institution. I feel like the institution is creating the environment for this to occur and then when it happens they don't deal with it or they punish you for coming forward. In my experience, the institutional rapes or the cover ups, the management practices, the slander, the gossip was more traumatic than the rape itself for me. I felt like they wanted to make me crazy or drive me to kill myself if I did not keep silent. It felt like a conspiracy of collusive acts where the military establishment was the perpetrator.
> I had more hatred for the Chief of Staff for the state national guard who was determining the outcome ... the outcome of what happened to MY BODY ... I had more hatred for him than I did for the man who raped me. People like him create the man who raped me. I can't explain it, it just seemed like being raped was just one part of the violence and trauma I experienced ... it is my reality ... as I experienced it.

According to Angela, elements of being in the military itself are triggers for her as well as for other military women who have experienced sexual violence. "I have friends who feel the same way I do. We are triggered when we wear the uniform, have a male supervisor, etc." She states that her betrayal by the military is similar to the betrayal of those who have been victimized by another institution.

> It's like the Catholic Church. Many survivors of sexual abuse cannot set foot in the Catholic Church because they feel betrayed by it. The institution is supposed to be loving and Christ-like but because their stories have been silenced for so long, they can no longer trust the organization. I'm not saying my experience is akin to the survivor of child molestation at the hands of the priest. I am just trying to understand where I am

coming from. The military has committed the worst act – betrayal. It has raped me too. So much for the whole caring about the soldier and putting soldiers first ... it's all about saving their reputation and sacrificing those of us like me ... hanging us out to dry.[63]

Sex trafficking

Sex trafficking is a modern form of slavery and is a major threat to women around the world. Women have become a low-cost and reusable commodity within the system of globalization. Unlike other "merchandise" that offer value only in a one-time sale, women can be sold again and again, and thus are becoming more popular than the illegal trafficking of guns and drugs. In addition, women can be trafficked cheaply by their exploiters; they are often manipulated into the industry with the promise of a good paying job in another country or forced with the threat of violence. The trafficker commits little or no capital to the enterprise and earns enormous profits while the trafficked women are violated, abused, and left with no escape.

The testimonies of Anita and Theresa are presented below.

Anita

After her husband had taken another wife, he became abusive and Anita was forced from her home. In order to support herself she began to sell vegetables from local farmers in the village market. While at the farmers' market Anita met a couple who offered her a banana and some water. After eating the banana, Anita felt ill; the couple offered her a pill and Anita took it. She lost consciousness and when she awoke she was on a train in an area she did not recognize. The man who had given her the pill told her he had tied drugs to her waist and that she must smuggle them for him. Feeling she had no choice, Anita did what the man said. He had also promised to pay her 20,000 rupees from the sale of the drugs and gave her directions to a place where she was to wait for him. She went to the meeting place, where she again encountered the man, and he turned her over to a woman, who took her to a house where she was held captive and forced to become a prostitute. According to her captor, Anita had been bought and she would have to work off her fee in the brothel. Anita was never told what that fee was.

> I insisted that I wanted to leave. The women began to slap me on the face. They cut off my hair. It was shoulder length in the back with short bangs in the front. Now that I had short hair, I knew that I could not leave the brothel without everyone identifying me as a prostitute. In my culture, short hair is the sign of a wild woman.
>
> For the next couple of days the women beat me often. They slapped me on the face and head with their hands and hit me about the waist and thighs with metal rods. I begged to be let go. I said that I wanted to

> return to my children in time for the biggest holiday of our culture. The women mocked me. They told me that if I worked with them for a couple of days, they would send me home with three bricks of gold and 30 to 40,000 rupees for the festival.

During her captivity, Anita was forced to bathe with the other women in the brothel several times a day. She was mocked repeatedly because of her modesty and forced to learn Hindi, the language of most of her customers. If she didn't know a word or was unable to speak the language, she was beaten.

> On the fourth day that I was in the brothel, my first client came to me. I refused to have sex with him. He had already paid so he grabbed me and tried to rape me. I fought him off. He had managed to get my clothes off but he was very frustrated because I was resisting him so much. He stormed out and asked for his money back. A couple of the brothel owners (voluntary prostitutes) came in and beat me. When they were done, the same man came back in. I then said that I would have sex with him only if he wore a condom. I knew about the need for condoms since I had learned that some of the other victims had very bad diseases. At first he refused but after another fight he finally agreed. By the time he left he had used three condoms.
>
> I only had one client my first day. But the next day, and every day after, I had three or four clients each day. I managed to get an ink pen. I would write messages to the police on the inside of cigarette boxes and send them out with my clients. Many clients promised to help but none did.
>
> Still, I was not able to go out to buy the condoms myself. In fact, for the entire month-and-a-half that I was in the brothel, I was never allowed to go out into the sun ... Downstairs there was a door that led outside. Several iron rods used for beating were leaned against the wall beside the door. One of the owners always guarded the door. Outside the door was a metal gate. When customers were not coming in and out, the gate was closed. The gate was held by a heavy chain that was locked by a large padlock.
>
> After serving clients for about eight days, an elderly man came to me as a client. When I was alone with him in the room, I told him that he was old enough to be my father. I told him, "I am like your daughter." I told him my story. He said that he had plenty of money and a Nepali friend. He promised to help me escape.

The client who promised his help later sent another man to gather information from Anita. Before he was able to help her, she found an opportunity to escape on her own and did. Once she fled the brothel she ran into two police officers who helped her get a taxi and she went to the house of the Nepali man who had promised to help her. Eventually, Anita was able to return home, but it was very difficult for her.

When I first went home to my family, it was very uncomfortable. The people in the village laughed at me. In my culture, a woman is scorned if she is missing for just one night. I had been missing for two months. It was very hard for my family, especially since we are members of the Brahmin caste. So, today I live in Kathmandu. I work as a domestic servant in the city. I am still without my children since they went to live with their father when I was taken away. I am told that my husband's new wife is very cruel to my children, but my husband does not want my children to be with me because of where I have been.

I know that my story will help other women who are forced into prostitution. Though I am grateful to be here to share my story, I am sad that I am not with my children – that my children cannot be here with me.[64]

Theresa

Theresa's story is one that involves acquaintance rape, gang rape, and trafficking. After being raped by Daniel, an older boy at her school, Theresa was devastated and felt she could tell no one. "Overwhelmed with shame, I chastised myself for being naive. For betraying myself. For betraying Jim [her boyfriend], my parents, and God … Guilt was suffocating … I berated myself with the same accusations I would later hear from others."[65]

Following the rape, Daniel told Theresa that his cousins were in the room while he raped her and had taken photos of the assault. He then said that his cousins were threatening to give the photos to Theresa's father, post them in school and church unless she complied with their requests and "earned" her photos back. Daniel took Theresa to meet his cousins and they threatened the safety of her family and told her she must submit to their demands.

> I didn't want to shame my family … I thought of the humiliation I would feel if the priest and kids at school saw those damning photos … mostly, I didn't want my father to learn I was no longer a virgin. I wanted to protect my mother and brothers while my dad was away traveling. To allow him to keep working there and keep our reputation safe.[66]

Feeling she had no choice, Theresa agreed to the cousins' terms. She was then forced on to a bed where she was gang-raped for hours.

> I don't remember how I ended up on the bed, but I remember Nick's weight pressing upon me, telling me to be quiet, forcing himself into me. Not only did I endure excruciating pain, but I was shocked at the brutality of the act. Before I could begin to recover from the assault, the quiet cousin was on me … Tears ran down my face … I was near unconscious when the torture stopped.

After the gang rape ended, Daniel drove Theresa home without the pictures. What Theresa had endured that night would become her routine several nights a week. She would sneak out of her home and was driven to different locations where men of all different ages paid the cousins to rape her. Theresa was gang-raped several times a week for the next two years, escaping only when her family relocated to another state.

> I felt that I couldn't tell anyone. I was terrified of the consequences. I believed I had no options. No choice. No free will ... I was brainwashed, confident that no one would believe my story if I told. Reduced to nothing inside, I was convinced that the welfare of my beloved family rested solely on my behavior. I was without hope, happiness, or future. Left only with shame ... I had been living in a zombie-like numbness ... At 17 years old, after having sex more times than I could count ... Terror was the only emotion for me that accompanied the base act.[67]

Reviewing each of these cases reveals the overwhelming suffering endured by women who experience rape as a result of both the violent act itself and the overarching culture. The following chapters will offer commentary on the testimonies of these women as they relate to the content of each section.

Notes

1. "Elizabeth Smart Speaks at Johns Hopkins University, May 6, 2013." Retrieved from: http://fox13now.com/2013/05/06/video-elizabeth-smart-speaks-at-johns-hopkins-university/.
2. Elie Wiesel, "The Holocaust as Literary Inspiration," in Elie Wiesel and Lucy Dawidowicz, eds., *Dimensions of the Holocaust* (Evanston: Northwestern University Press, 1977), p. 6.
3. Rebecca Chopp, "Theology and the Poetics of Testimony," in Delwin Brown, Sheila Greeve Davaney, and Kathryn Tanner, eds., *Converging on Culture: Theologians in Dialogue with Cultural Analysis and Criticism* (New York: Oxford University Press, 2001), p. 56.
4. Ibid.
5. Susan J. Brison, "Surviving Sexual Violence," in Stanley G. French, Wanda Teays, and Laura M. Purdy, eds., *Violence against Women: Philosophical Perspectives* (Ithaca: Cornell Press, 1998), pp. 12–13.
6. Equality Now, "Pakistan: The Hudood Ordinances – Denial of Justice for Rape: The Case of Dr. Shazia." *Women's Action* 26(1). Retreived from: http://www.equalitynow.org/take_action/pakistan_action261.
7. Nancy Venable Raine, *After Silence: Rape and My Journey Back* (New York: Three Rivers Press, 1998), pp. 9, 22.
8. Ibid., pp. 19–20.
9. Ibid., p. 22.
10. Ibid., pp. 23–24.
11. Ibid., pp. 26–27.
12. Ibid., p. 26.
13. Ibid.

14 Andrea Benton Rushing, "Surviving Rape: A Morning/Mourning Ritual," in Mary Odem and Jody Clay-Warner, eds., *Confronting Rape and Sexual Assault* (Wilmington: Scholarly Resources, 2003), pp. 6–10.
15 Ibid., p. 7.
16 Ibid., pp. 6, 11.
17 Robin Warshaw, *I Never Called it Rape: The Ms. Report on Recognizing, Fighting and Surviving Date and Acquaintance Rape* (New York: Harper & Row, 1988), p. 4.
18 Ibid.
19 Ibid., pp. 5–6.
20 Ibid., p. 7.
21 Ibid., pp. 16–17.
22 Ibid., pp. 30–31.
23 Charlotte Pierce-Baker, *Surviving the Silence: Black Women's Stories* (New York: W.W. Norton and Company, 1998), pp. 89–91. Ruth shared her story twenty years after her rape.
24 Ibid., p. 93.
25 Ibid., p. 91.
26 Lee Madigan and Nancy C. Gamble, *The Second Rape: Society's Continued Betrayal of the Victim* (New York: Lexington Books, 1989), pp. 39–43.
27 Marital rape is currently legal in Afghanistan, the Bahamas, Brunei Darussalar, Ethiopia, Honduras, Kenya, Mongolia, Nigeria, Pakistan, Sri Lanka (except in cases of separation), Sudan, Yemen, and Zambia.
28 Raquel Kennedy Bergen, *Wife Rape: Understanding the Response of Survivors and Service Providers* (Thousand Oaks, CA: Sage Publications, 1996), pp. 12–13.
29 Ibid., pp. 14, 33.
30 Ibid., p. 15.
31 Ibid., pp. 21, 44.
32 Ibid., pp. 21, 27.
33 Ibid., p. 33.
34 Ibid., p. 56.
35 Ibid., p. 16.
36 Ibid., p. 43.
37 Ibid., p. 52.
38 Ibid., p. 26.
39 Ibid., pp. 53, 42.
40 Brownmiller, p. 187.
41 Ibid.
42 Peggy Reeves Sanday, *Fraternity Gang Rape: Sex, Brotherhood, and Privilege on Campus* (New York: New York University Press, 1990), pp. 99–101.
43 Lara Setrakian, "Saudi Rape Victim Tells Her Story: Victim to Receive Whipping and Jail for Being in Nonrelative's Car When Attacked." Retrieved from: http://abcnews.go.com/International/story?id=3899920&page=1.
44 Shahla Haeri, "The Politics of Dishonor: Rape and Power in Pakistan," in Mahnaz Afkhami, ed., *Faith and Freedom: Women's Human Rights in the Muslim World* (New York: Syracuse University Press, 1995), p. 169.
45 Khalid Ahmed, "The Sociology of Rape." *Slogan* February (1992), pp. 36–37.
46 Mukhtar Mai, *In the Name of Honor* (New York: Washington Square Press, 2006), pp. 8–12.
47 Ibid., pp. 18–19.
48 Ibid., pp. 23–25.
49 Ruth Seifert, "War and Rape: A Preliminary Analysis," in Alexandra Stiglmayer, ed., *Mass Rape: The War against Women in Bosnia-Herzegovina* (Lincoln: University of Nebraska Press, 1994).

60 *Learning from women's testimony*

50 Sharon Frederick and the Aware Committee on Rape, *Rape: Weapon of Terror* (River Edge: Global Publishing Company, 2001), p. 5.
51 Human Rights Watch Women's Rights Project, *The Human Rights Watch Global Report on Women's Human Rights* (New York: Human Rights Watch, 1995), pp. 17–19.
52 Jan Ruff-O'Herne, *50 Years of Silence* (Sydney: Tom Thompson, 1994), pp. 64–106.
53 Ibid., p. 127.
54 Ibid., p. 136.
55 Jan Goodwin, "Sierra Leone is No Place to be Young." *New York Times*, February 14, 1999.
56 UNIFEM, *Women on the Frontline – Democratic Republic of Congo* (Canberra: Australian Development Cooperation, 2008).
57 Nancy Gibbs, "Sexual Assaults on Female Soldiers." *Time*, March 8, 2010.
58 Note that 22 percent of women reported sexual harassment, 27 percent of women reported sexual assault, and 11 percent reported being raped. See Lane Evans, "News release." House Committee on Veterans' Affairs: Democratic Office. Retrieved from: http://veterans.house.gov/democratic/press/109th/9-29-05mst.htm.
59 "Harman Introduces Bipartisan Bill to Halt Rape and Sexual Assault in the Military." July 29, 2008. Retrieved from: http://harman.house.gov/2008/07/July29-MST.shtml.
60 PBS, "Survivors Share Experiences of Sexual Assault in the Military." March 13, 2013. Retrieved from: http://www.pbs.org/newshour/bb/military/jan-june13/sexualassualt_03-13.html.
61 Rebekah Havrilla, "Hearing Testimony of Rebekah Havrilla before the Military Personnel Subcommittee of the Senate Armed Services Committee." March 13, 2013. Retrieved from: http://www.armed-services.senate.gov/statemnt/2013/03%20March/Havrilla%2003-13-13.pdf.
62 Madigan and Gamble, pp. 55–59.
63 A. Hope and M. Eriksen, "From Military Sexual Trauma to 'Organization-Trauma': Practicing 'Poetics of Testimony.'" *Culture & Organization* (15)1 (2009): pp. 109–127.
64 Polaris Project, "Testimony of Anita." Retrieved from: http://actioncenter.polarisproject.org/the-frontlines/survivor-testimonies/38-testimonies/56-testimony-of-anita.
65 Theresa Flores, *The Slave across the Street: The True Story of How an American Teen Survived the World of Human Trafficking* (Boise: Ampelon Publishing, 2010), pp. 48–51.
66 Ibid., pp. 54, 59.
67 Ibid., pp. 117, 105.

4 A preliminary analysis of sexual violence and rape culture

> It is astonishing that in all our worlds of feminism and anti-sexism we never talk seriously about ending rape. Ending it. Stopping it. No more. No more rape.
>
> Andrea Dworkin[1]

Rape culture is a cyclical system where rape is viewed as inevitable and is accepted as a fact of life and impossible to change. Rape culture is a widespread epidemic and women around the globe suffer as the objects of its oppression. Prevailing attitudes of patriarchal culture and the manifestation of rape culture within society instigate and perpetuate gendered violence, plaguing women with the injustice of the violation of their human rights.

In the Steubenville rape case – or what has become known simply as "Steubenville" – a sixteen-year-old girl was repeatedly raped by two high school football players while others watched, took photos, tweeted, and shared the assault on Facebook. It is a case that perfectly exemplifies rape culture in the twenty-first century. Now, victims are shamed not only in their own communities but on the global stage, thanks to social media.

Following her rape, Jane Doe quickly found herself being judged harshly by friends, classmates, Steubenville community members, and persons around the world who commented via Twitter, Facebook, the evening news, and so on. People questioned why Jane Doe was intoxicated; they questioned why she would put herself in such a vulnerable position. Others attacked her verbally, while some threatened her, demanding that she not file charges.

Many were concerned for the two young men who were charged in the case. They were two of Steubenville high school's football greats. Once the boys were convicted, many others were saddened, distressed, angry, and once again took to social media, this time to lament the verdict. CNN reporter Poppy Harlow commented that it was "incredibly difficult ... to watch as these two young men who had such promising futures, star football players, very good students, literally watched as they believed their life fell apart."[2]

Rape culture promotes, supports, and condones the prevailing attitudes presented throughout this case. The futures of males are viewed as the foundation of society whereas the dignity and humanity of women and girls are of little concern. As Laurie Penny states,

> What makes these men so sure of their inviolable right to stick their fingers and cocks into any part of any female they can hold down that they actually make and distribute images of each other doing so? Rape culture. That's what rape culture is – The cultural acceptance of rape.[3]

Defining rape

In order to address rape culture and the devastation caused by sexual violence properly, it is necessary to define what sexual violence is and discuss its societal functions. While there have been multiple attempts to define rape, many have been and remain problematic. Accordingly, I will begin by identifying sexual violence and offering a proper definition of rape which will be followed by an explanation of how rape functions within society.

Stemming from the Latin word rapere, meaning "to take by force," rape has traditionally been defined inappropriately, and historically legal definitions have been limited in scope. English common law defined rape as taking place only when the vagina was penetrated by a penis with force and ejaculation occurred.[4] In addition, rape traditionally has been defined by common law as taking place when a man has "intercourse with a woman not his wife; by force or threat of force; against her will and without her consent."[5] Both of these definitions are problematic for multiple reasons and fall far short of defining the violent act of rape properly. According to these definitions, wives cannot be raped, forceful anal and oral penetration do not qualify as rape, and the use of other body parts or objects to rape does not equate to rape. In addition, these definitions deny that men and children can also experience rape.

Although current definitions have expanded these limited and problematic attempts to identify the nature of rape, an archaic ideology of sexual violence continues. The Uniform Crime Report (UCR) – the FBI's annual report of crime statistics – defines rape as "the carnal knowledge of a female forcibly and against her will."[6] This definition, adopted in 1927, also excludes multiple sexual assault acts, including forced anal and oral penetration, the use of other body parts or objects to rape, and the use of drugs or alcohol to facilitate rape. Moreover, it denies that men and children can be raped, and it dismisses coercion.

Recognizing the problematic nature of this definition, the US Department of Justice and the National Crime Victimization Survey expanded the definition of rape to include "attempted rapes, male as well as female victims, and both heterosexual and homosexual rape."[7] Nevertheless, as with the UCR's definition, multiple other factors involved in rape are not taken into consideration. As Frances Reddington and Betsy Wright Kreisel explain, "Even though, a number of governmental agencies have expanded their definition of rape, their definitions still remain limited in scope."[8]

Looking outside of the US, other nations also present vague and incomplete definitions of rape.[9] For instance, Brazil's definition is similar to the UCR's. According to Article 213 of the Brazilian Penal Code, rape is defined as "constrain[ing] a woman to the bodily carnal knowledge, by means of violence or serious threat."[10] Article 177 of Japan's Penal Code states that "A person who, through violence or intimidation, has sexual intercourse with a female person of not less than thirteen (13) years of age commits the crime of rape."[11] Article 131 of the Criminal Code of Russia defines rape as "sexual relations with the use of violence or with the threat of its use against a victim or other persons, or in taking advantage of the victim's helpless condition."[12] Meanwhile, the United Kingdom has sought to rid its legal system of ambiguities: the Sexual Offences Act 2003 claims that rape occurs only via "penile penetration."

Rape laws in Pakistan are particularly problematic due to General Zia's alteration of the legal system in 1979 to make it in accordance with Islamic law. Rape was removed from the standard penal code and included under the Offence of Zina Ordinance, which is a sub-category of the Hudood Ordinance of 1979. With this alteration, rape (*zina-bil-jabr*) is included with various types of sexual activity, such as adultery, and is a religious offense "subject to [a] different standard of evidence and punishment and the appellate jurisdiction of Islamic higher courts."[13] Previous rape laws in Pakistan, which were also problematic, defined rape as compulsory sexual intercourse; however, the Zina Ordinance[14] is even more troublesome in that it restricts the circumstances where rape can have taken place and has removed both statutory rape[15] and marital rape as crimes. In Pakistan, rape is now an offense that can occur only outside of marriage.

The failure to define the act of rape properly is widespread, and this is representative of the influence of rape culture. According to each of these definitions, several of the cases presented in the previous chapter do not qualify as rape. When defining rape, we must offer a comprehensive definition that acknowledges these women's experiences and testimony. A proper definition must acknowledge that the act of rape can be perpetrated in multiple ways. Thus, rape must be understood as the vaginal, anal, or oral penetration of any person, including spouses, children, other family members, and acquaintances, with any body part or object, without consent. In addition, it must be recognized that in order to consent, one cannot be coerced, threatened, or be under the influence of any substance. Thus, submission or non-resistance do not equate to consent.

Functions of rape

While society in general has commonly confused the act of rape with sex, rape in fact has little to do with sex. Instead, rape is a violent act that is used to dominate, control, and humiliate. Susan Brownmiller drew attention to this idea in her groundbreaking work *Against Our Will: Men, Women, and Rape*. She argues,

> Man's discovery that his genitalia could serve as a weapon to generate fear must rank as one of the most important discoveries of prehistoric times, along with the use of fire and the first crude stone axe. From prehistoric times to the present, I believe, rape has played a critical function. It is nothing more or less than a conscious process of intimidation by which all men keep all women in a state of fear.[16]

In agreement with Brownmiller, Ruth Seifert explains, "studies show that rape is not an aggressive manifestation of sexuality, but rather a sexual manifestation of aggression."[17] She explains that, according to the popular myth known as "the pressure cooker theory of male nature," rape is the result of an uncontrollable male drive.[18] This myth claims that men are not responsible for their actions; instead, they are victims of their own uncontainable and instinctive nature. However, this myth is exactly that – a myth, a falsehood. Rape has very little to do with nature or sexuality. As Fortune explains,

> There have been years of indoctrination that in "sex crimes" there are rapists who cannot control themselves and victims who really want to be raped. In this erroneous stereotype, sexual violence is seen as being primarily sexual in nature ... Any victim of rape knows that she has experienced the most violent act possible short of murder.[19]

Thus, rape is an extremely violent act that is a product of power and control, implemented by sexual means.

Some have argued against this treatment of rape and claim that instead rape is about sex and must be identified as such. According to Catherine MacKinnon,

> While intending the opposite, some feminists have encouraged and participated in this type of analysis by conceiving rape as violence not sex. While this approach gave needed emphasis to rape's previously effaced elements of power and dominance, it obscured its elements of sex ... if it's violence not sex why didn't he just hit her?[20]

To answer MacKinnon's question, the perpetrator is not only seeking to harm his victim physically, but also to dominate, control, humiliate, and wound their spirit. There is no doubt that perpetrators of domestic violence and other forms of physical violence against women seek to dominate and control their victims. However, when a woman is raped, she is not only dominated and controlled, but often experiences shame and ultimately feels rejected by her community as a result of the rape culture. Katie described feeling rejected and blamed by her mother, causing her to feel even more ashamed. Angela stated that the treatment she endured from the military was worse for her than the actual rape. Anita stated that she was rejected by her community, and her children were no longer allowed to be with her because she had been trafficked. "Qatif Girl" was physically punished by her brother and he attempted to kill her because she had been raped.

In addition, the emotional and spiritual wounding resulting from a rape is so deep that it often leaves the woman feeling that she has experienced a death, or worse. Mukhtar explained that "rape is the ultimate weapon"; she stated that the rape itself had killed her and that she felt dead in the eyes of others. Jan stated that the rape was "worse than dying." Susan and Nancy both described feeling dead in some sense and Lori recounted living in a zombie-like existence. Dr. Shazia, "Qatif Girl," and Mukhtar all felt that their communities were calling upon them to commit suicide.

In many of the testimonies, the women stated that they felt they were at fault for their rapes and therefore could not tell anyone about their victimization; they feared that the judgment, humiliation, and shame they felt for themselves would then also come from others. Robin, Lori, and Rachel each stated that they felt they must keep their rapes a secret. According to Debbie, she felt she would receive no support from her family and had no choice but to remain silent. Theresa stated she felt such guilt and shame that she could tell no one about the repeated rapes she was enduring.

Also negating the idea that rape is about sex is the reality that in many cases rape serves no sexual purpose for the perpetrator. In fact, studies have demonstrated that perpetrators often experience sexual dysfunction while committing the act of rape.[21] This is also well demonstrated by the testimonies in Chapter 3. B. described this, explaining that when her rapists where unable to perform the act physically they would use other objects to rape her. Debbie recounted a similar experience, stating that her husband raped her using a hairbrush, a broken bottle, and other objects. This violent act is an expression of rage as well as domination over the woman. For the perpetrator, the goal is to humiliate, degrade, and achieve control by forcing the woman to submit; thus, sexual means are utilized to commit this violent act but the act is not sex. As Alice Vachss explains, those who "think rape is about sex" confuse "the weapon with the motivation."[22]

Furthermore, while MacKinnon questions rape as violence rather than sex, rapists have also stated that they utilized rape as an act of violence to dominate and control. For instance, one rapist recounted that after offering to help a woman whose car had broken down, he beat and raped her as a means of revenge. He stated, "The rape was for revenge. I didn't have an orgasm. She was there to get my hostile feelings off on."[23] Another serial rapist stated that he raped because he believed women thought they were better than him. "Rape was a feeling of total dominance. Before the rapes, I would always get a feeling of power and anger. I would degrade women so I could feel there was a person of less worth than me."[24]

According to Timothy Beneke, men commonly consider rape to be a counterattack against a woman who has first "attacked" a man with her weapon of provocative appearance. "Jay," who was interviewed by Beneke, describes this:

> As a man you're taught that men are more powerful than women, and that men always have the upper hand, and that it's a man's society; but then you see all these women and it makes you think "Jesus Christ, if we have all the power how come all the beautiful women are telling us what to buy?" And to be honest, it just makes me hate beautiful women because they're using their power over me ... In this society, if you ever sit down and realize how manipulated you really are it makes you pissed off – it makes you want to take control. And you've been manipulated by women, and they're a very easy target because they're out walking along the streets, so you can just grab one and say, "Listen, you're going to do what I want you to do," and it's an act of revenge against the way you've been manipulated.[25]

Rape is an act of torture; there is no more brutal an attack upon the dignity and intimate self of a person. To invade the interior of someone's body is a form of torture by any measure. The act of rape results in physical pain, humiliation, and shame, as well as loss of self-respect, autonomy, and identity. As Andrea Dworkin explains, "struggle for dignity and self-determination is rooted in the struggle for actual control of one's own body, especially control over physical access to one's own body."[26] Sexual and personal identities are closely intertwined, thus sexual violence attacks the personal self. According to Seifert, "in most cases the rape victims themselves experience the act not as a sexual one, but as an extreme and humiliating form of violence against person and body, accompanied by an intense fear of dying."[27]

Rape must be understood as functioning as a violent act. Sexuality is not at the center of the perpetrator's act; instead, rape and other forms of sexual violence against women derive from abhorrence and the intention to dominate and control. As Seifert states,

> In seeking the societal functions of rape, everything points to the conclusion that it regulates the unequal power relationships between the sexes: it serves to maintain a certain cultural order between the sexes or – when this order becomes fragile – to restore it.[28]

Rape culture

A rape culture is one in which rape and other forums of sexual violence are common and widespread. In addition, sexual violence is condoned, normalized, and encouraged by prevailing norms and attitudes and misogynistic practices are validated and rationalized through various acts of sexism. According to Robert Jensen,

> [Ours] is a culture in which sexualized violence, sexual violence, and violence by sex are so common that they should be considered normal. Not normal in the sense of healthy or preferred, but an expression of the sexual norms of the culture, not violations of those norms. Rape is illegal, but the sexual ethic that underlies rape is woven into the fabric of our culture.[29]

In a rape culture, although there is a high prevalence of rape and sexual violence, there is a low instance of prosecution and conviction. Victim blaming is commonplace and those who have been raped suffer community rejection in some fashion. Images of sex and violence are intertwined and imagery of violence against women is rampant. In a rape culture women do not have the benefit of full legal, economic, and social equality with their male counterparts; instead, women are seen as inferior and deserving of the violence perpetrated against them.

There are many contributing factors to the existing rape culture. From our assigned gender roles, to the language we use to refer to men and women, to the myths we hold, to society's treatment of those who are sexually victimized, various elements of our society participate in building a structure that encourages, supports, and perpetuates a culture of violence against women.

Rape culture: a social evil

When discussing sexual violence and rape culture, evil is an important element to be included in the larger conversation. There are different types of evil: evil that we do, also known as moral evil; and evil that we experience, also known as social evil. The former refers to deliberate acts against others and the latter is not chosen but rather is an evil that is systemic and present in the social structures that facilitate it. Whereas some forms of evil are quickly condemned, others are intertwined within our "culture, education, and religion – events or behaviors regarded as normal, common, even good – it is not easy to spot evil's presence even when we suspect it is there."[30]

Although the traditional categories of "moral" and "natural" are generally utilized to classify evil, Nel Noddings argues that a third category of social or "cultural" evil must be recognized to describe evil that is generated by established and accepted cultural norms embedded within the "tissues of society."[31] Whereas natural evil serves to identify suffering endured as a result of illness, death, and other tragedies that occur because of natural causes, and moral evil – or sin – represents deliberate acts perpetrated by individual agents, social evil includes various conditions that result from social structures, such as racism, classism, ageism, poverty, war, and sexism.[32]

As Noddings explains, men throughout history have not engaged in patriarchy with the intent of leaving their female family members helpless and separated from their society. Rather, "Human beings frequently participate in the practices of their culture without reflective evaluation."[33] Generally, we do not believe we are committing evil when we engage in particular social structures; our deeds are not deliberate individual acts, but rather those that are brought about by the larger social structures and cultural norms.

Rosemary Radford Ruether also acknowledges that evil, in addition to being personal, is social and historical. Although these aspects are different, they are highly interconnected.

> Sin always has a personal as well as a systemic side. But is never just "individual": there is no evil that is not relational. Sin exists precisely in the distortion of relationality, including relation to oneself. Although there are sins that are committed primarily as personal self-violation or violation of another individual – abuse of one's body by intoxicants, rape, assault, or murder or another – even these very personal acts take place in a systemic, historical, and cultural context.[34]

Ruether goes on to explain that

> Powers and principalities exist as the precondition of evil choices. But, these powers and principalities are precisely the heritage of systemic social evil, which conditions our personal choices before we choose and prevents us from fully understanding our own choices and actions.[35]

Rape culture is a historical and systemic social evil that shapes our thoughts and behaviors and conditions our choices. Thus, because rape culture exists and is perpetuated by societal and cultural norms, it must be recognized as a social evil.

Social evil is embedded in the flesh of our society and is particularly dangerous because it is "bigger than any of us or all of us as individuals ... The system transcends us as individuals in space and time. It forms an organizational structure of society and social ideology which is itself the product of many centuries and generations."[36] Thus, social evil is powerful and has a life of its own and functions to inflict pain and suffering on particular groups and individuals. It is an evil that resists eradication; although it changes forms, sometimes cosmetically and sometimes more significantly, it remains strong. Gerda Lerner explains this phenomenon with respect to the oppression of women, stating,

> Traditionalist defenses of male supremacy based on biological-deterministic reasoning have changed over time and proven remarkably adaptive and resilient. When the force of the religious argument was weakened in the

nineteenth century the traditionalist explanation of women's inferiority became "scientific."[37]

This category of evil is particularly important for women who experience sexual violence and are isolated from the larger society as a result. The consequence of such evil leaves victims experiencing their suffering as personal and not shared with the larger social heritage. Thus, the sense of isolation and alienation is amplified. In addition, social evil leaves victims in a position to blame themselves. As a member of the larger society, women who endure sexual violence have learned the culture of blaming from early on; thus, they experience a unique victimization not perpetrated by other crimes.

Today, we continue to engage in the rape culture without recognizing our complicity. We teach our daughters to be passive and our sons to be aggressive; we perpetuate myths about sexual violence; we teach our daughters not to get raped rather than teaching our sons not to rape. The social evil of our societal structures calls us to do these things, and generally we do them without thought or reflection.

To say that rape culture is a social evil is not to disregard personal accountability and responsibility for our moral choices. While we must acknowledge the social evil of our cultural norms, as Ruether explains, we must also "sort out our appropriate responsibility ... to recognize both the difference and interconnection between individual and social evil."[38] Men who choose to objectify women and rape, among other acts of violence, commit a moral evil. Likewise, women who choose to blame victims of sexual violence and participate in society's "second rape" are committing a sin. According to Ruether,

> Women sin by cooperating in their own subjugation, by lateral violence to other women who seek emancipation, and by oppressing groups of people such as children and domestic servants under their control. Women can be racist, classist, self hating, manipulative toward dominant males, dominating toward children. But these forms of female evil cooperate with and help to perpetuate an overall system of distorted humanity.[39]

Every person who chooses to participate in the distortion of the relationship between self and other engages in moral evil. Thus, women are complicit in the rape culture. They have been socialized into the myths and norms and have been induced to collaborate with them. This said, it must be acknowledged that women have not created and nor are they the primary perpetuators of such evil. Likewise, it must also be acknowledged that women who are victimized and feel guilt, shame, or self-hatred as a result of assault are themselves not committing moral evil. Rather, these feelings are symptomatic of the ongoing victimization perpetrated by the larger rape culture.

Elements of rape culture

Gender

Traditional sex roles are polarized, demanding specific behaviors of each gender, and sexuality is prescribed and proscribed for men and women. Women are taught to be passive and men aggressive. Men have been labeled as sexual subjects, understood as predators; and women as sexual objects, understood as prey. According to Brownmiller, women are trained to be rape victims. She states that simply to learn the word "rape" is to be trained in the power relationship between men and women. In fact, girls learn from an early age that girls are raped while boys are not.[40] Although boys and men certainly have been and are subjected to sexual violence, statistics show that 92 percent of rape victims are female and 99 percent of perpetrators are male.[41] In addition, as Brownmiller explains, often when men are raped, the act is committed against them in order to humiliate and treat them like women. Thus, rape becomes understood as having to do with gender.

Generally speaking, masculinity signifies culturally defined characteristics for men which constitute maleness according to the socio-historical environment. Within rape culture masculinity equates to power, control, superiority, and dominance. It defines manhood and is achieved through behaviors that are problematic and often physically aggressive and threatening. Rape becomes a means of demonstrating masculinity and "putting women in their place." While not all men are rapists, Timothy Beneke explains that all men grow up learning to "think like a rapist, to structure his experience of women and sex in terms of status, hostility, control, and dominance."[42] According to Myriam Miedzian, "when dominance and power define masculinity, men rape as a way of putting 'uppity' women in their place."[43]

Studies of male college students offer startling statistics about willingness and desire to commit sexual violence. In a study that was administered to 3,862 university students, 25 percent of male students admitted to committing at least one, and in some cases many, attempted rapes.[44] Another study completed by Neil Malamuth revealed that one in three male students stated that if all chances of being caught were removed, they would commit rape. In addition, 26 percent of men admitted to committing forceable sexual acts and attempted rapes that resulted in the woman crying, pleading, screaming, fighting, and other observable forms of distress.[45]

According to Andrew Merton, "For many adolescent males just out of high school, the transition to college represents a first step in a struggle for a kind of 'manhood' from which women are viewed as objects of conquest – worthy, but decidedly inferior adversaries."[46] In addition, Miedzian explains that college administrators commenting on the high rates of gang rape on college campuses stated that if men refuse to participate in rape their masculinity will be questioned and they run the risk of being labeled "wimp" or "gay."[47] Thus, violent male sexual behavior must be understood as confirming manhood.

Michael Kimmel states that there are four traditional rules of American manhood:

- It is never acceptable to display any feminine qualities or "sissy stuff"; manhood repudiates and devalues all femininity.
- Manhood is measured by power, wealth, and success.
- Men must not be emotional or reveal their feelings.
- Manhood requires risk-taking and aggressive behavior.[48]

According to Kimmel, these four rules result in a male sexuality that is built upon "scoring" or having intercourse with as many partners as possible, taking risks, and being emotionally distant. Women are socialized to the role of asexual gatekeeper and the male's job is to wear down her resistance. Kimmel argues that men suffer from "socialized deafness" that strikes only when women say "no." He explains,

> Men's fear of being judged a failure as a man in the eyes of other men leads to a certain homosocial element within the heterosexual encounter: men often will use their sexual conquest as a form of currency to gain status among other men. Such homosocial competition contributes to the strange hearing impairment that men experience in any sexual encounter, a socialized deafness that leads us to hear "no" as "yes," to escalate the encounter, to always go for it, "to score."[49]

Masculinity demands that men be aggressive, in control, and have power over women. Men view their behavior as "either idiosyncratic or situationally appropriate and thus it reduces their sense of moral responsibility for their actions."[50] Because sexual behavior confirms manhood, men view women as objects to conquer and sex as a commodity to be obtained by whatever means necessary. This social construction encourages rape while providing excuses and justifications for sexual violence.

Language

Language also plays a significant role in supporting gender roles; the way we describe men and women and the way we talk about sexual violence support the overall rape culture. According to Helen Benedict, there is a language of rape that "portrays women as sexual, subhuman, or childlike temptresses, and that perpetuates the idea of women as legitimate sexual prey."[51] She states that rather than describing rape as violence, this language describes it as an act of pleasure or comedy. The language of rape is a significant element of rape culture and can be easily identified in daily life. Looking at various news reports about sexual violence, journalists, whether intentionally or not, have participated in rape culture. In these accounts, words utilized for female victims include "pretty, hysterical, attractive, flirtatious, bright, bubbly, petite, pert, vivacious, girl (for grown woman)."[52] In a violent gang-rape story – the brutal attack against a woman who became known as the "Central Park Jogger" – terms employed to describe the assault included "fondled, caressed, and had sex with."[53]

This language of rape is dualistic. As Benedict explains, these words used to characterize how women have been sexually assaulted would never be used to describe men. In addition, whereas women are often referred to as "girls," men are never referred to as "boys." Terms used to describe the rape itself are representative of the language that a rapist would use to justify his actions as consensual and nonviolent. Consequently, this language of rape is utilized to deny the seriousness and brutality of rape and ignores the woman's experience while downplaying the rapist's actions.

Rape myths

Rape myths are stereotypical and prejudicial falsehoods that are believed about rape, victims of rape, and rapists, and they are central to this overall topic of rape culture. There is no crime more difficult to prove than rape and no victim is trusted less than the one who has been raped. This is a direct result of the numerous myths that have gripped society and are widely accepted as truth. These fabrications have been given the status of "myth" with the purpose of denoting that they are not simply untruths, but function to reveal the "structure of meaning permeating a particular culture."[54] Myths enable the establishment of hierarchies and form homogenized communities through the defining of standpoints and transformation of commonly held presumptions into supposed "objective truths." This results in myths becoming accepted as reality.

Rape myths have become commonplace catchphrases that function severely to damage women who have suffered sexual violence. Bourke explains that these falsehoods result in sexual torture becoming situated in the realm of moral edification. She states, "they enable individuals (such as perpetrators) to place their actions in a framework that is recognizable by others (such as potential victims) while withdrawing legitimacy from people (actual victims, for instance) who wish to contest them."[55] Thus, recognizing the suffering of women who are targeted by these myths is necessary in order to lay bare their primary function, which is to "reduce the lived experiences of specific individuals to undifferentiated bodies."[56]

Of course, all rape myths are extremely problematic and contribute greatly to the overall rape culture. However, different myths have different functions. As mentioned earlier, the "pressure cooker theory" claims rape is the result of an uncontrollable male sex drive in order to excuse the act and define it as one of sex rather than violence. That being said, other myths function to blame women for their victimization and contribute to the suffering endured following a rape. The classic myth "no woman can be raped against her will" is one method among many utilized to shift blame from the rapist to the victim.

It implies several fallacious notions, including that women instigate their rape, women want to be raped, women enjoy rape, and only women who are physically assaulted during an attack are raped. Each of these erroneous but pervasive ideas functions to perpetuate the rape culture and causes women who are victimized to condemn themselves.

According to Brownmiller, the idea that no woman can be raped against her will "is not intended to encourage women to do battle against an aggressor – rather, it slyly implies that there is no such thing as forcible rape – and that it is the will of women to be ravished."[57] "She was asking for it" is a common claim made by both rapists and the rape culture to excuse the act itself and place blame on the victim. Women are scrutinized for their behavior, mannerisms, chosen attire, location, etc. This is well demonstrated by Reis's comments regarding the rape of Tamar. She claims that Amnon is not guilty of rape, but rather that Tamar is guilty of seducing behavior that ultimately leads to her submitting to intercourse. Carmichael and Aalders similarly claim that Dinah was "willing" because she went out of her home by herself. Looking to the contemporary testimony presented in Chapter 3, Lori and Amy each experienced their rapists claiming that the women either wanted or enjoyed the assault and "asked for it." Amy specifically discussed feeling she was partially to blame for her rape. Lori questioned herself and wondered if her going on the date and consenting to kissing instigated her rape.

The idea that women who are not physically assaulted or beaten are not raped is one that has far-reaching roots. For instance, Deuteronomy 22:23–24 states that

> If there is a young woman, a virgin already engaged to be married, and a man meets her in the town and lies with her, you shall bring both of them to the gate of that town and stone them to death, the young woman because she did not cry for help in the town.

This passage is one that greatly influences the rape culture by implying that if a woman is truly being raped, some sort of a struggle must occur; if no struggle takes place, the only reasonable conclusion is that the woman consented and was a willing participant.

Katie's testimony demonstrates this experience of being judged by the culture because a weapon or "violent" assault was not involved in her rape. She stated that, following her rape, she felt it was necessary to lie and claim that she was threatened with a weapon for fear that she would not be believed. She also explained that she lied to her mother because she believed her mother would have been angry with her if there was not a weapon involved in the rape. Katie stated that once she revealed that no weapon was involved in her rape, her mother was angry and did not believe her daughter's rape was traumatic. According to Katie, her mother blamed her for the rape and Katie felt ashamed.

An additional myth that perpetuates the rape culture and functions to silence victims is the misguided notion that women falsely report rapes. While false accusations do occur, they transpire at the same rate as other falsely reported crimes – about 2 percent.[58] Thus, the idea that women "cry rape" and have the reputations of men at their disposal is erroneous. Nevertheless, women are greatly affected by this myth and often do not report their rapes (to legal authorities or family, peers, counselors, etc.) for fear that they will not be believed. Rachel expressed this in her testimony when she stated, "No one would have believed me if I said anything. I wouldn't have dreamed of saying anything."[59] Likewise, Katie feared that if she reported who had raped her and how, she would not be believed and thus felt it was necessary for her to contrive a story about a stranger with a weapon. Throughout her ordeal, Katie described feeling as if she was not believed and was being punished for reporting the rape.

Rape myths are strategies that function to marginalize women further and generate sympathy for the rapist. They are utilized by society to deny the reality of rape, dismiss incidents of sexual violence, and condemn the victim. Rape myths teach women to feel guilt, shame, and blame for their own victimization and allow rapists to commit sexual violence virtually immune from any punishment. It is through these myths that women come to know that rape is the worst thing that could happen in life, that they must work to avoid being raped, and that if they are so careless as to be raped, their life will become nothing more than a shameful existence.

Media

In the widely televised (twenty-six countries) *General Hospital*, Luke and Laura fell passionately in love after Luke violently raped Laura. The storyline unfolded to reveal that Luke had professed his love for Laura, who was married and unwilling to accept his advances; however, because his passion was so great, he was unable to control his lustful desires and raped her. Following the rape, Luke was Laura's only source of solace, and he comforted her, assuring her that she should not feel guilty. After Luke helped Laura to heal from her emotional wounds, she left her husband to marry him. Surprisingly, or maybe not, Luke and Laura have become the soap opera industry's most celebrated romantic couple. This particular example well demonstrates how the media supports and encourages rape myths and perpetuates rape culture. As millions tune in daily to witness the ongoing love affair between Luke and Laura, they are indoctrinated to believe that women want to be raped, women enjoy rape, men should understand "no" as "yes," and men rape because they themselves are victims of their own uncontrollable urges.

It is impossible to overstate the influence of the media and its reinforcement of the prevailing rape culture. In today's society, children spend more time surrounded by Facebook, Twitter, television, film, video games, music, magazines, etc. than they do in the classroom or with their parents. We are inundated with a daily barrage of various forms of media that image violence against women as sexy and the norm. Advertisements are a major source of imagery of women being presented as objects to be used, abused, and thrown away. Regardless of product type, from Dolce & Gabbana to Carl's Jr., the sexualization of women is continually used to market goods. Music that promotes the domination of women through sexual violence controls the air waves. "Blurred Lines" by Robin Thicke has lyrics that have been dubbed "rapey," and the song has been banned from college campuses because of its misogynistic nature; yet it was still a number-one hit. Pornography is rampant and has become the number-one addiction in the world, surpassing, drugs, alcohol, and gambling. The examples are endless.

Media's contributions to rape culture continue to grow and evolve over time. The Steubenville case clearly demonstrates the many ways in which social media has become a major contributor to supporting the overall culture of sexualizing and objectifying women. Another serious offender is hentai – an extreme form of pornography presented in cartoon format that is available in various forms of media, including computer games, comic books, and online "entertainment." Its use in Japan is widely accepted and it is easily accessible through a quick search of the internet. Rape, incest, and other forms of sexual violence are common themes of hentai.

In 2006 a new rape-simulator video game called "RapeLay" was released in Japan. It was quickly listed on Amazon and could be found on shelves around the world for purchase. The object of the "game" is to take revenge on a girl for having made a report against the "player" for sexual molestation. The scenario takes place on a subway platform and with the click of a mouse different methods of assault can be chosen – from groping, to lifting her skirt, to rape. The "player" can follow the girl on to the train, where he can also rape her mother and sister and hear each repeat the line "I want to die." Each woman can also be gang-raped or raped in different locations, including a public restroom, a park, and a hotel. The ultimate goal is to conquer each woman and convert her into a compliant sex servant who enjoys being raped. A website for the game described the three female "characters" in the following way:

Manaka: A younger girl with short black hair who wears a blue dress. She moans a lot more than the other characters and tends to look at the player with fearful cute eyes during sex. The player can make her wear cat ears so that she will produce cat noises.

Aoi: A brunette girl with long hair who wears a schoolgirl uniform. She is more resistant than both of the other characters. Her hair ornament is optional.

Yuko: A brunette women with a green shirt and large breasts and is a lot older than the other two characters. Yuko can wear glasses to make her produce different sound effects.[60]

The descriptions of each of these women are as disturbing as the concept of "Rapeplay." Clearly, this "game" functions as a media form of terrorism against women. It encourages the normalization of sexual violence and renders women nothing more than objects to be dominated. Although international outrage led to its being banned in multiple countries, including the US, the "game" is still easily available for free download on the internet.

Media plays a significant role in supporting and perpetuating the rape culture. Through its various forms, the media promotes the social construction of masculinity, reinforces rape myths, and encourages violence against women. Its methods of supporting this culture continue to grow. As long as these images and concepts of violence against women are accessible through the media, society will accept rape as the norm.

The second rape

Masculinity, rape myths, the media, and rape language all work hand in hand to support a rape culture that encourages violence against women, dismisses sexual violence, and victimizes women multiple times over. This elaborate system functions to keep women in a state of fear, believing that no worse possible thing could happen in their lives than rape. For women who are raped, this system leaves them feeling ashamed and at fault for their own victimization. As a result, victims of rape are "twice damned" and experience what is best described as a "second rape."

Women who have experienced sexual violence are silenced by the rape culture and treated differently from any other victim of crime. As discussed earlier, rape victims experience rejection by their community; they are blamed for their victimization and shamed by society. In some cases, victims of sexual violence are either called upon to commit suicide or have family members attempt to murder (or succeed in murdering) them in order to preserve family honor. All of the twenty-five testimonies presented in Chapter 3 discuss struggling with the after-effects of rape that are directly related to the rape culture and the responses they anticipated encountering or actually received from the overall society as well as loved ones, police, medical personnel, court officials, etc.

Rather than being heard, taken seriously, and offered justice, in many cases women who are raped are burdened with proving the rape occurred. For instance, in a recent rape case, Ken Buck, a prosecutor in Colorado, told a rape victim that although the police had recommended felony charges – because her rapist had admitted that she said "no" and she was intoxicated, unable to resist, and unconscious during part of the assault – her case would not be prosecuted. Buck stated that, because she had a previous sexual relationship with the rapist and invited him into her home when she was drinking, a jury would likely find her case was nothing more than "buyer's remorse."[61]

It is no surprise that rape is the most underreported crime across the board. Victims who have chosen to voice their pain by sharing with others, seeking medical attention, filing a police report, or pursuing prosecution open themselves to scrutinization by the public and various institutions that are supposed to support and protect them. According to Andrew Park Sung, "Reporting a rape is equivalent to suicide. Laid bare to the scrutiny of voyeurs by the media, the victim is, in effect, forced to splay her legs before the public eye."[62]

Medical treatment: a continued rape

"Don't shower" is generally the first thing a rape victim is told. If there is any hope of prosecuting the rapist, evidence must be preserved. Certainly, a rape exam is necessary in order to collect evidence to support a prosecution. However, the overall process of receiving medical attention is often experienced as a continuation of the rape itself. Women who choose to obtain medical help are frequently left to wait for hours, sometimes in crowded waiting rooms, and often alone, before they are treated. The rape exam is an incredibly invasive procedure that can be painful and humiliating. Instead of offering emotional support and tending to the woman's physical injuries, unless severe, the hospital functions as an extension of the police department and focuses on collecting evidence. While seeking medical attention is crucial following a rape, in doing so, women feel powerless and as if their rape is continuing.

Although Susan, Dr. Shazia, and Nancy each experienced what has been labeled "real rape" by society, they each endured a second rape, beginning with their medical treatment. Susan recalls feeling as if she were a "piece of meat." Rather than treating her as a woman who had just been brutally victimized, the doctors simply gave her orders and poked and prodded her without any concern for her emotional wellbeing. In fact, Susan had to demand a gown; it had not even occurred to the doctors that she may be uncomfortable standing naked in front of two men just after being raped.

Nancy had a similar experience to Susan's. She stated that after sitting alone for what felt like an eternity and being denied the opportunity to rinse her mouth because it held evidence, her body itself was treated as evidence. She did not feel that her body was her own; instead, it had become "the scene of the crime." In addition, she stated that while she convinced herself that the rape exam was necessary and worth the pain she would endure, once it began, she felt differently.

> A female doctor comes in for the pelvic exam. I am not sure I can go through with it. There is evidence inside me. They need it. The pain of the instrument inside me will be worth it, I tell myself. If it hurt some more, they will catch him. When the speculum enters me, I bite my lip. When it opens inside me, I do not think it is worth it.[63]

Dr. Shazia's experience with medical treatment was different from Susan's and Nancy's, but it was an assault nonetheless. Although she was a doctor herself, Dr. Shazia was at the mercy of the physicians she saw in the hospital. She was told by her doctors not to report her rape because of the shame that it carried. Her wounds were not treated, she was denied access to her family, and instead was sedated and sent to a psychiatric hospital. The manifestation of rape culture within Pakistan meant that Dr. Shazia's rape shamed her family; thus, her physicians believed the only appropriate treatment was to address her mental health and prevent her from reporting the crime.

Raped by law

Police, detectives, prosecutors, and other law enforcement officials are not immune to the rape culture and are influenced by the myths, language, and media in the same way as general society. Thus, all elements of the rape culture come into play when a rape is reported. Investigators participate in the system by putting the victim on trial before deciding whether or not her report should be taken seriously. The victim's personal life is scrutinized and she is judged for her sexual behavior, manner of dress, personality, location, etc. Regardless of the type of rape endured, be it stranger or acquaintance rape, victims are treated with the same misgivings. While other crimes are reported without immediate suspicion of the victim, rape is unique in that the victim must prove her own innocence before her victimization is taken seriously.

In addition to being treated as criminals themselves, rape victims must endure the gruesome task of recounting the details of their rapes. Reliving each painful moment is something that any victim of crime would experience while making a report to the police or following up with investigators and prosecutors, or giving testimony in court. However, for victims of rape, this process results in re-victimization. Not only are they reliving a painful memory, but they are repeating how they were violated, degraded, and humiliated while at the same time being judged, blamed, and shamed by those who are supposed to protect them. Furthermore, because the rape culture teaches women that rape is the result of their own foolishness and the worst thing that can happen in a woman's life, victims recount their brutal assaults with feelings of guilt and shame.

In a study completed about law enforcement's treatment of rape cases,[64] police officers were quick to comment about how they felt about investigating reported rapes. One officer stated that a rape victim's credibility could be judged by her attractiveness, depending on to whom she reported her rape. Another explained that it did not matter whether a rape had actually occurred; much more important was whether the prosecutor could build a case. He explained,

> A woman had gone to her employer's house to play cards. She got drunk and passed out. Upon regaining consciousness, the woman discovered she had had intercourse but didn't remember giving her consent. A woman like this who's been drinking or taking drugs would not make a credible witness. I didn't encourage her to prosecute. She may have been violated, but the district attorney wouldn't have liked this case.[65]

While one officer admitted that women never ask to be raped, he stated that there is a specific type of woman who is ignorant and thus culpable. "We call her HUA for 'head up her ass'. She's unable to sever former destructive relationships ... she likes to get attention."[66] A female police officer stated, "I get frustrated with the women. They've usually made bad decisions in life. In two years, I haven't seen a legitimate rape yet. Most of what I see is prostitutes."[67] Hence, it seems that rather than focusing on evidence and objective facts, law enforcement officers investigate rape cases based on a "system that caters to the archaic myth that only certain women get raped."[68]

The police mirror the attitudes of society. A study of jury trials demonstrated that juries have an inclination to be prejudiced against the victim and the prosecution in rape cases. According to Madigan and Gamble, "They will go to great lengths to be lenient with defendants if there is any suggestion of contributory behavior on the part of the survivor, including hitchhiking, dating, and talking with men at parties."[69]

In many of the testimonies presented in Chapter 3, the women chose not to report their assaults for these very reasons. Rachel stated that she did not think anyone would believe her. Theresa discussed feeling such guilt and shame that she could not bring herself to tell anyone, knowing that if her family, friends, and pastor found out, they would be ashamed of her. Susan, who did report her rape, recalled recognizing that she was spared the insult that many rape victims endure because she was raped by a stranger and was visibly injured. However, she also noted that her credibility was still an issue because the rapist claimed she provoked the attack. Thus, the police encouraged her to discuss her love and concern for her husband within her deposition. Susan also explained that she was shocked to see that the police began her report with "Since I am athletic ... " in order to explain why she would have gone for a walk by herself.[70]

Sally also discussed her ordeal with the police and felt that her complaint was not taken seriously. Because her husband was her rapist, the police discouraged her from pressing charges. Although she asked to have a rape kit done, they refused. When she asked to speak to a woman, she was told none was available. After going to the state police to report the rape, Sally stated that she was totally "embarrassed" as the detectives purposefully humiliated her by making her repeat details several times and asking her specific questions that were irrelevant and designed only to cause her further embarrassment.

Although law enforcement agencies and prosecutors are supposed to work towards justice for victims of crime, because of the prevailing rape culture, these institutions also participate in justifying rape and violence against women. Victims who choose to report their rapes are ultimately judged and blamed. The entire process of seeking justice results in the reinforcement of cultural attitudes that women should feel ashamed and blame themselves for their victimization.

Conclusion

We live within a culture where rape has been repeatedly misidentified. Men are socialized to rape; myths are constructed to protect the interests of the culture; and social institutions, language, and the media are tools to reinforce the culture. Consequently, women who are raped endure the brutal attack, are treated as evidence by medical personnel, and are persecuted by law enforcement agencies. In addition, they are "raped" again by the general society, including the people they think of as loved ones. Society judges rape victims with a harshness that is reserved only for them, as no other crime victim is treated in this way. In addition, when a rape occurs and is reported, despite the woman's need for privacy, feelings of security, and dignity, very often every aspect of her life is exposed by the media. As Park explains, "The media capitalizes on the victim's suffering until it – and she – are used up."[71]

Rape is not about sex. It must be understood as a weapon against women and one that is utilized to control, dominate, and humiliate. The weapon of rape itself, coupled with the overarching rape culture, functions to wound women physically, emotionally, and spiritually. This unchanging culture is a major contributor to the ongoing assault experienced and the massive suffering endured by the victims of sexual violence.

Notes

1 Andrea Dworkin, "I Want a Twenty-four Hour Truce during Which There is No Rape," in Emilie Buchwald, Pamela Fletcher, and Martha Roth, eds., *Transforming a Rape Culture* (Minneapolis: Milkweed, 1993), p. 11.
2 See Winston Ross, "CNN Feels Sorry for Steubenville Rapists; World Can't Believe its Ears." The Daily Beast, March 18, 2013. Retrieved from: http://www.thedailybeast.com/articles/2013/03/18/cnn-feels-sorry-for-steubenville-rapists-world-can-t-believe-its-ears.html.
3 Laurie Penny, "Steubenville: This is Rape Culture's Abu Ghraib Moment." *New Statesman*, March 19, 2013. Retrieved from: http://www.newstatesman.com/laurie-penny/2013/03/steubenville-rape-cultures-abu-ghraib-moment.
4 See Ann Clark, *Women's Silence, Men's Violence: Sexual Assault in England 1770–1845* (New York: Pandora, 1987).
5 Susan Estrich, *Real Rape: How the Legal System Victimizes Women Who Say No* (Cambridge, MA: Harvard University Press, 1987), p. 8.
6 Department of Justice: Federal Bureau of Investigation, "Appendix II: Offenses in Uniform Crime Reporting," in *Crime in the United States* 2004. Retrieved from: http://www2.fbi.gov/ucr/cius_04/appendices/appendix_02.html. For a recent discussion of the problematic nature of this limited definition, also see Roxann MtJoy, "The FBI's Shockingly Narrow Definition of Rape." September 15, 2010. Retrieved from: http://womensrights.change.org/blog/view/the_fbis_shockingly_narrow_definition_of_rape.
7 See Department of Justice: Bureau of Justice Statistics, "Rape and Sexual Assault." 2009. Retrieved from: http://bjs.ojp.usdoj.gov/index.cfm?ty=tp&tid=317.
8 Frances Reddington and Betsy Wright Kreisel, *Sexual Assault: The Victims, the Perpetrators, and the Criminal Justice System* (Durham, NC: Carolina Academic Press, 2005), p. 7.
9 Note that it is impossible to present every country's definition of rape due to space limitations in this study; thus, here I will present definitions from several countries

around the world in order to demonstrate that the misidentification of rape is a global issue.
10 See Interpol, *Brazilian Penal Code, Article 213*. Retrieved from: http://www.interpol.int/public/Children/SexualAbuse/NationalLaws/csaBrazil.asp.
11 Interpol, *National Laws: Japan*. Retrieved from: http://www.interpol.int/Public/Children/SexualAbuse/NationalLaws/csajapan.asp.
12 See the Criminal Code of the Russian Federation, "Crimes against Sexual Inviolability and Sexual Freedom of the Person. Article 131: Rape." Retrieved from: http://www.russian-criminal-code.com/PartII/SectionVII/Chapter18.html.
13 Human Rights Watch, *Crime or Custom: Violence against Women in Pakistan* (New York: Human Rights Watch, 1999), p. 33.
14 See Sections 3 and 19 (3), Offence of Zina Ordinance, 1979.
15 Statutory rape was defined as intercourse with a girl under the age of fourteen, regardless of consent.
16 Brownmiller, p. 15.
17 Seifert, p. 55. Also see Renee Kasinsky, "Rape: A Normal Act?" Canadian Forum September (1975): pp. 18–22; Diana Russell, *The Politics of Rape* (New York: Grune and Stratton, 1975); Peggy Reeves Sanday, *The Socio-Cultural Context of Rape* (Washington, D.C.: United States Department of Commerce, 1979).
18 Seifert, p. 55.
19 Fortune, p. 5.
20 Catherine MacKinnon, "Sexuality, Pornography, and Method: Pleasure under Patriarchy." *Ethics* 99(2) (January, 1989): p. 323.
21 Studies have demonstrated that perpetrators often experience sexual dysfunction while committing the act of rape, thus supporting the assertion that rape is not about sex, but rather violence, power, and control. See Ann Wolbert Burgess *et al.*, *Sexual Assault of Children and Adolescents* (Lanham: Lexington Books, 1978); I. Brownes, "Assailants' Sexual Dysfunction during Rape: Prevalence and Relationship." *Medicine, Science, and the Law* 31(4) (1991): pp. 322–328; Nicholas Groth, "Motivational Intent in Sexual Assault of Children." *Criminal Justice and Behavior* 4(3) (1977): pp. 253–264; Nathaniel McConaghy, *Sexual Behavior: Problems and Management* (New York: Plenum Press, 1993).
22 Alice Vachss, *Sex Crimes: Ten Years on the Front Lines Prosecuting Rapists and Confronting Their Collaborators* (New York: Random House, 1993), p. 78.
23 Diana Scully and Joseph Marolla, "'Riding the Bull at Gilley's': Convicted Rapists Describe the Rewards of Rape," in Patricia Searles and Ronald Berger, eds., *Rape and Society: Readings on the Problem of Sexual Assault* (Oxford: Westview Press, 1995), p. 63.
24 Ibid., p. 64.
25 Timothy Beneke, "Jay: An 'Armchair' Rapist," in Searles and Berger, eds., p. 56.
26 Andrea Dworkin, *Pornography: Men Possessing Women* (New York: Plume, 1991), p. 243.
27 Seifert, p. 56.
28 Ibid., p. 57.
29 Robert Jensen, "Cruel to be Hard: Men and Pornography." Sexual Assault Report Spring (2004): p. 54.
30 Ivone Gebara, *Out of the Depths: Women's Experience of Evil and Salvation* (Minneapolis: Fortress Press, 2002), pp. 2–3.
31 Nel Noddings, *Women and Evil* (Berkeley: University of California Press, 1989), pp. 104–105.
32 Ibid., pp. 120–121.
33 Ibid., p. 104.
34 Rosemary Radford Ruether, *Sexism and God-Talk: Toward a Feminist Theology* (Boston: Beacon Press, 1983), p. 181.

35 Ibid., pp. 181–182.
36 Mary Potter Engel, "Evil, Sin, and Violation of the Vulnerable," in Susan Brooks Thistlethwaite and Mary Potter Engel, eds., *Lift Every Voice: Constructing Christian Theologies from the Underside* (San Francisco: Harper & Row, 1990), p. 164.
37 Gerda Lerner, *The Creation of Patriarchy* (New York and Oxford: Oxford University Press, 1986), p. 18, cited in Noddings, p. 105.
38 Ruether, p. 181.
39 Ibid., pp. 165, 180.
40 Brownmiller, p. 309.
41 See the Department of Justice: Bureau of Justice Statistics at http://www.ojp.usdoj.gov/bjs/.
42 Timothy Beneke, *Men on Rape: What They Have to Say about Sexual Violence* (New York: St. Martin's Press, 1982), p. 16.
43 See Myriam Miedzian, "How Rape is Encouraged in American Boys," in Buchwald *et al.*, eds., pp. 153–163.
44 Mary Koss and Cheryl Oros, "Sexual Experiences Survey: A Research Instrument Investigating Sexual Aggression and Victimization." *Journal of Consulting and Clinical Psychology* 50(3) (1982): pp. 455–457.
45 Neil Malamuth, "Rape Proclivity Amongst Males." *Journal of Social Issues* 37(4) (1981): pp. 138–157.
46 Andrew Merton, "On Completion and Class: Return to Brotherhood." Ms. Magazine, September 1985, quoted in Warshaw, p. 107.
47 Miedzian; also see Sanday, Fraternity Gang Rape.
48 See Michael Kimmel, "Clarence, William, Iron Mike, Tailhook, Senator Packwood, Spur Posse, Magic ... and Us," in Buchwald *et al.*, eds., pp. 119–138.
49 Ibid., pp. 127–128.
50 Scully and Marolla, p. 61.
51 Helen Benedict, "The Language of Rape," in Buchwald *et al.*, eds., p. 103.
52 Ibid., p. 104.
53 Ibid.
54 Joanna Bourke, *Rape: Sex, Violence, History* (Berkeley: Shoemaker Hoard Publishing, 2007), p. 24.
55 Ibid.
56 Ibid.
57 Brownmiller, p. 312.
58 See the Department of Justice: Bureau of Justice Statistics.
59 Warshaw, p. 31.
60 See "RapeLay." Wikia. Retrieved from: http://gaming.wikia.com/wiki/Rapelay.
61 Scot Kersgaard, "Buck's Refusal to Prosecute 2005 Rape Case Reverberates in US Senate Race." *Colorado Independent*, October 11, 2010. Retrieved from: http://coloradoindependent.com/63491/bucks-refusal-to-prosecute-2005-rape-case-reverberates-in-u-s-senate-race.
62 Andrew Sung Park, *From Hurt to Healing: A Theology of the Wounded* (Nashville: Abingdon Press, 2004), p. 40.
63 Raine, p. 28.
64 See Madigan and Gamble.
65 Ibid., p. 72.
66 Ibid., p. 74.
67 Ibid., pp. 74–75.
68 Ibid., p. 73.
69 Ibid., p. 75.
70 Brison, p. 16.
71 Park, p. 41.

5 Sexual violence, *han*, and spiritual death

> When trust is lost, traumatized people feel that they belong more to the dead than to the living.
>
> Judith Lewis Herman[1]

The idea that rape is a fate worse than death is one that has long existed. Looking to the biblical rape texts and purity legends presented in Chapter 2, it is clear that society's valuing of a woman's chastity over her life is a deeply rooted concept. Dinah, Tamar, and David's pilegesh were all perceived as shameful, unworthy of marriage, and of little value following their rapes. Maria Goretti, as well as the other virgin martyrs discussed, chose death over rape in order to preserve her purity as a means of demonstrating her love for God. Lucretia committed suicide in the belief that it was the only way to redeem her honor. The common theme of experiencing feelings of wanting to die after being raped found in the testimony of contemporary women in Chapter 3 well demonstrates that this notion continues to exist in our culture today.

Beyond these texts, the abusive nature of Christian theological teachings contributes to exacerbating the suffering endured by those who experience sexual violence, particularly women who practice the Christian faith. Victims suffer not only because of the rape, but also because of the reaction of their community and their own feelings of shame and self-blame, which are encouraged by the prevailing culture. The best way to describe this suffering is "han," a Korean concept and term that describes the compression of multiple sufferings that damage the spirit. This concept is appropriate to articulate the anguish endured by victims of sexual violence because it encompasses the multiplicity of sufferings that torment women following a brutal assault. In addition, it acknowledges the ongoing spiritual wounding that can ultimately result in a spiritual death.

Spiritual death

In order to understand what spiritual death is, it is necessary first to discuss what spirituality is and how it should be defined. Spirituality refers to the interior life and mystical[2] experience of the individual. It is

> the binding force of the unity between the inner and outer life ... the all-pervading divine energy and seamless web of oneness intimate to life

itself. Creation is not alone, separate from its source, but deeply and mysteriously imbued with spirit in every aspect of mind, soul, and matter.[3]

Ewert Cousins states, "The spiritual core is the deepest center of the person. It is here that the person experiences ultimate reality."[4] Also upholding this emphasis of one's inner relationship to her or his "ultimate reality," Sandra Schneiders contends that spirituality should be understood as "a fundamental dimension of the human being ... and the lived experience which actualizes that dimension."[5] Thus, spirituality is not only constitutive of the person, but can also be developed and articulated through the activities associated with spirituality in the individual's life, in addition to the entirety of the life of faith which includes political, social, and bodily dimensions. Accordingly, spirituality is not only the individual's life in relation to the divine; rather, it is the person's life lived in the divine.

Schneiders also asserts that a "generic" spirituality is non-existent. Instead, spirituality is determined by the focus of the individual's life. She explains that spirituality is

> the experience of consciously striving to integrate one's life in terms not of isolation and self-absorption but of self-transcendence toward the ultimate value one perceives. It is progressive, consciously pursued, personal integration through self-transcendence within and toward the horizon of ultimate concern.[6]

While spirituality has frequently been associated with otherworldliness and opposition to the body, it must be understood as striving towards goodness and righteousness within the world. "Spirituality unifies the tension between mind and heart, body and soul, and inner and outer life ... [It] is the awareness of the oneness that underlies duality and difference, as each outward action reveals the interconnected presence of the holy."[7] Thus, a spiritually aware temperament is marked by feelings of empathy, compassion, and oneness with life.

Noting this understanding of spirituality, it must be recognized that abusive theological teachings damage a woman's sense of self. Dualistic thinking within the Christian tradition has long demeaned the body and nature in favor of the spirit and the mind, associating women with the former and men with the latter. Rita Nakashima Brock explains,

> Aspects of femaleness that most compel attention to an embodiedness that is linked to vulnerability and feeling, menstruation and birthing, for example, are regarded in male-dominant societies as unclean and defiling. Rejection of the body's vulnerability is also a necessary attribute for warriors in patriarchal societies, a skill taught to those in basic training in the military. Hence, things that lead away from or conquer the body – a strong will, spirituality, and intellect, for example – are prized as higher ways to truth.[8]

The body has been claimed to be "the home of evil, the prison of the soul, needing continual castigation for the benefit of the spirit."[9] Saints of the Church have been noted for despising their physical existence. Female saints have had particular tendencies towards masochistic behavior. For instance, St. Margaret Mary Alacoque described cleaning up vomit with her tongue, feeling joy after filling her mouth with an ill man's excrement, and holding her lips against the Sacred Heart of Jesus for three hours, for which she was rewarded. Daly explains,

> It should be noted that the self-defiling acts of these feminine saintly masochists are acts of self-denying flight, not from their own desire, but from natural disgust. They are attempts at self-purification as the saints perceived this to be required of them by a male god. Moreover, these women were accurate in their assessment of the male god's demands. It is significant that the god–man Jesus is believed to have rewarded Alacoque immediately for swallowing the male patient's excrement. It is equally significant that the church legitimated this behavior and this fantasy by officially promoting the veneration of the sacred heart.[10]

The result of this damaging charge against the female nature has been the subordination of women. The patriarchal anthropology of the Christian tradition has declared woman the cause of sin, sinful in nature, and woman's subjugation has been deemed her punishment. This is well represented in the stories of Pandora, Lilith, and Eve, which portray women as antagonists of peace and harmony and claim woman is the origin of evil. As Rosemary Radford Ruether explains, "The female comes to represent the qualities of materiality, irrationality, carnality and finitude, which debase the 'manly' spirit and drag it down into sin and death."[11] Recognizing her body as damaged and morally corrupt, a woman's spirit is also wounded.

Also problematic is the central message of redemptive suffering. Christianity is a primary force in shaping the acceptance of abuse. The right to care for ourselves becomes interpreted as in conflict with following the ways of Christ, and self-sacrifice and obedience become understood as the definition of a Christian identity. According to Daly,

> The qualities that Christianity idealized, especially for women, are also those of a victim: sacrificial love, passive acceptance of suffering, humility, meekness, etc. Since these are the qualities idealized in Jesus "who died for our sins," his functioning as a model reinforces the scapegoat syndrome for women.[12]

Our culture calls for the sacrifice of women by naming their roles as caretakers and nurturers of the family. "Women's self development is sacrificed to the family and this sacrifice is considered redemptive for all involved, including the woman."[13] The perception of sacrifice as being positive in the

Christian tradition supports the teaching of girls and women to be self-sacrificing in social circumstances and becomes intertwined with social beliefs that women are sacrificial. Likewise, bodily suffering as spiritually redemptive is equated with the Christian idea of "denial of the body." Women's bodies are disconnected from the notion of redemption and, thus, integrity and worth. Adams explains,

> by failing to provide a prophetic word against interpretations that, on one hand, justify domination and, on the other, reinforce subordination, the church becomes complicit in perpetuating these images and ideas so ripe for misapplication. The church becomes a party to dominant–subordinate relationships.[14]

A woman's spirituality is at the core of her being; however, it is damaged as a result of abusive theological teachings. Claims that women are sinful, that bodies are corrupt, and that suffering is redemptive are certainly wounding as they disregard the true nature of the spirit. This, coupled with the violation and invasion of her body, attack upon her dignity and personal self, followed by societal blame, silencing, and shame, results in a disconnect with the true self. Self-determination is quashed and self-transcendence becomes very difficult. The societal imaging of a rape victim, caused by rape culture, creates the self-image of a woman as depraved, soiled, damaged, and unworthy. The continued experience of *han* and inability to release the multiple sufferings endured slowly murder the spirit. As any serious wound that goes untreated presents the possibility of death, deep spiritual wounds that are continually exacerbated by one's own self-image present the possibility of a spiritual death.

For the woman who is victimized by rape, re-victimized by society, and ultimately loses her own self-worth as a result, spiritual death is a likely consequence. With such a depraved self-image and continual assault on the perception of self perpetrated by the culture, she can no longer see herself in relation to the divine.[15] While she is physically alive, spiritually she is dead.

Han

The Korean concept of *han* can be understood as "a festering wound generated by unjust psychosomatic, social, political, economic, and cultural repression and oppression."[16] This concept is significant because it represents not a singular feeling, but rather many feelings that are compressed together and interact with one another to generate a particular *han* depending on the circumstances. Because *han* is an intricate concept, it is difficult to define in a complete way. This being said, in an effort to illuminate *han*, Suh Nam-Dong has defined it as "the suppressed, amassed and condensed experience of the oppression caused by mischief or misfortune that forms a kind of lump in one's spirit."¹⁷ According to Hyun Young-Hak, *han* can be understood as

> a sense of unresolved resentment against injustice suffered, a sense of helplessness because of the overwhelming odds against, a feeling of total abandonment, a feeling of acute pain of sorrow in one's guts and bowels making the whole body writhe and wiggle, and an obstinate urge to take "revenge" and to right the wrong all these constitute.¹⁸

Han is the suffering experienced by those who are innocent and, according to Park, can be described as a "void of grief." He states,

> When grief surpasses its sensibility line, it becomes a void ... not a mere hollowness, but an abyss filled with agony ... As the long or sharp agony turns into a dark void, the void swallows all the other agendas of life, intensifying its hollowness.¹⁹

Its characteristics include being comprised of multiple afflictions and being engendered by unjust social structures. *Han* is the experience of those who are voiceless and marginalized, a suffering that is "meaningless"²⁰ and one that functions only to destroy the individual, leaving her or him with no power.

Chung Hyun Kyung has given special attention to *han*, recognizing it as the "most prevalent feeling among Korean people."²¹ She explains that *han* arises out of a "sense of impasse," and is particularly experienced by women. She states,

> Often Korean people, especially the poor and women, have not had any access to public channels through which they can challenge the injustices done to them. They have long been silenced by physical and psychological intimidation and actual bodily violence by the oppressor. When there is no place they can express their true selves, their true feelings, the oppressed become "stuck" inside. This unexpressed anger and resentment stemming from social powerlessness forms a "lump" in their spirit. This lump often leads to a lump in the body, by which I mean the oppressed often disintegrate bodily as well as psychologically.²²

Han can be experienced both individually and collectively, and, depending on the circumstance, can be either passive or aggressive. Each of these dimensions has two levels: conscious and unconscious. Within the personal dimension at the conscious level, *han* can be expressed as resignation or as vengeance and the will to revenge; whereas at the unconscious level, *han* is hidden by feelings of powerlessness and resentment. Within the collective dimension at the conscious level, *han* is conveyed through communal anguish and the will to revolt. The unconscious level of *han* is expressed through sexual, racial, and religious indignation.²³

On a collective basis, social injustice in all its forms, which impacts the oppressed as a whole, escalates the communal *han*. "When the oppressed undergo suffering over several generations without release, they develop a collective unconscious *han* and transmit it to their posterity."[24] While this is similar to the concept of "collective unconscious"[25] developed by Carl Jung, Jung views the collective unconscious as universal whereas the collective unconscious of *han* is specific to a particular group or persons. In addition, from generation to generation of the oppressed, *han* intensifies.

Han *of the rape victim*

Because *han* is characterized as a multiplicity of suffering, situation specific, meaningless, and caused by unjust social structures, it is an appropriate term and concept to describe the suffering experienced by the rape victim. It identifies her experience as more than an issue of theodicy or as a distinctive suffering that cannot be experienced in other circumstances. In addition, *han* identifies the rape victim's suffering as destructive, having no value, and resulting from rape culture (the actual rape occurs because of rape culture and the continued assault is perpetrated by rape culture). Furthermore, the concept of *han* acknowledges the deep spiritual wounding generated by sexual violence.

While the rape victim can suffer either an aggressive or a passive *han*, within this study I am focused on the experience of a passive *han* because it is this that can ultimately result in a spiritual death. As Park explains,

> Passive *han* takes the form of heart rending resignation. It lets go of everything, including the self. The self is so poorly developed that its organizing center is diffuse, and the soul moves toward self-disintegration ... If one's resigned *han* is deep seated, it can hurt one even to the point of death. Self-denigration, low self-esteem, self-withdrawal, resignation, and self-hatred are conspicuous marks of passive *han*.[26]

The depth of this *han* is often hidden from others because of "embarrassment, shame, guilt, and repression."[27] When the rape victim suffers passive *han*, rather than seeking vengeance against her rapist, vengeance is sought against herself.

The suffering of the rape victim does not simply encompass traditional theodicy questions of how to speak about the divine in the midst of suffering. The victim is not necessarily concerned with whether or not the divine is omnipotent, benevolent, or omnipresent. Rather, the victim is concerned about her own ability to see herself in relation to the divine. Because of the feelings of immorality that have been thrust upon her by the community, she no longer feels capable of embodying the divine. The concern is focused directly on the perception of self rather than on the divine's ability to have kept the rape from occurring or to end the suffering endured.

Suffering has been defined as a common – even universal – experience; however, the experience of the rape victim is drastically distinct from suffering incurred as a result of other circumstances and is not one that non-rape victims can fully relate to. *Han* allows for this understanding and also permits the communication of a particular experience among rape victims due to their common experience. Finally, *han* does not focus on a single type of suffering; rather, it encompasses the multiplicity of suffering endured simultaneously by women who experience sexual assault. It symbolizes the cry of rape victims as oppressed people and acknowledges the structural oppressions that create and perpetuate this overall torment of the woman's inner self. Thus, *han* should be understood as different from the traditional concept of suffering and a more suitable term to describe the experience of the rape victim.

Victims of rape experience *han* on a collective level as well as an individual level. The victim is part of the larger group of women who have experienced sexual assault and community rejection due to rape culture and oppression which results in the collective experience of *han*. In addition, a collective unconscious experience of *han* is suffered as a result of the ongoing compressed *han* of multiple generations; the *han* of rape victims suffered over thousands of years is transmitted to their posterity.

Rape, compounded by the second assault of the societal response, results in the individual experience of *han* that Park describes as "the will to revenge, resignation, regret, diffuseness, absence, bitterness, and helplessness, reacting to a private oppression that can also often be connected to collective and structural oppression."[28] Rape culture blames the victim and seeks to silence her, which creates an additional suffering beyond the rape itself. It is this element that distinguishes rape from other forms of violence. For the rape victim, it is the intertwined experience of the rape itself and the response of the community which causes the shame and self-blame that constructs her *han*; this *han* is what murders her spirit.

Rape culture and the construction of han

In a rape culture, girls are told from a very young age that rape is the worst possible thing that could happen in their lives. They are told that if they are raped, their lives will be destroyed and they will become impure. Those who are raped are told that feeling dirty is natural. These societal messages set women up to experience these feelings if raped and prepare them to be "collapsible women." In addition, they are left with the impression that there is no other "healthy response other than to break down."[29]

In a rape culture, a woman's chastity is valued over her life. This is well demonstrated by the stories of Lucretia and Maria Goretti. As discussed in Chapter 2, Lucretia committed suicide in order to redeem her honor, stating, "As for me, I am innocent of fault, but I will take my punishment. Never shall Lucretia provide a precedent for unchaste women to escape what they deserve."[30] In addition, her suicide was praised by Tertullian and Jerome;

lifting up Lucretia's story as an example, rape was explained as the one exception that calls for suicide.

Maria Goretti became a mythic figure and was canonized as a saint by the Catholic Church for protecting her virginity,[31] and her life-threatening rape was referred to as "an attractive pleasure."[32] Had Maria been raped and then murdered, the idea of her being considered for sainthood would have been laughable. Likewise, this theme is present in the Acts of Paul and Thecla. Thecla accepts that she is condemned to face the beasts; however, she petitions that she not be held in prison while awaiting the sentence so that she can avoid being raped and remain pure. Her condemners agree with her that her chastity is of great importance and grant her request; but her death sentence remains intact.

Furthermore, as discussed in Chapter 4, women who are raped are routinely blamed by society and accused of causing their own victimization. The community responds to their brutal assault with rejection rather than support, leaving the victim feeling shamed and isolated. One woman explains:

> The aftermath was almost as bad as the act itself. When people read about the rape in the papers I was actually shunned, even in church. The women whispered behind my back. They thought I must have brought the rape upon myself. Some even asked me why I didn't fight back. Months passed before the gossip subsided ... Even my husband listened to those voices. The pastor? He did not know how to handle the situation. He never said anything to me. Never.[33]

The examination of women's stories in religion illuminates this facet of rape culture as both Dinah and Tamar are blamed for their rapes. Moreover, in the women's contemporary testimony presented in Chapter 3, victim blaming was a common theme. Both Lori and Rachel were blamed by their rapists and thought that if they reported the assaults, they would not be believed. Likewise, Amy was repeatedly told throughout her rape that she "wanted it," and Katie was called a liar and blamed for her assault by the military and even her own mother.

Victims of rape are not listened to as they attempt to express their experiences of sexual assault; rather, they are inundated by accusations and antagonistic messages about themselves from persons and organizations of authority. In addition, they are forced to keep silent. "The rules of the abuser, the court, the church, and the racist patriarchal culture can forbid a woman to interrupt her established order by naming the torment she has endured."[34] Multiple women described feeling that they were forced to be silent about their rapes. For instance, Dr. Shazia was silenced by law enforcement as well as medical personnel. Both Angela and Katie described feeling that they had been raped a second time by the military and were punished for coming forward. Sally was repeatedly silenced by law enforcement officers. She explained that her complaints were ignored or not taken seriously and that the officers repeatedly tormented her by asking embarrassing questions and mocking her.

To sum up, rape culture normalizes the victimization of women on multiple levels and leaves victims of rape feeling ashamed, isolated, silenced, and unable to articulate their own experiences. This cultural assault results in the victim experiencing additional anguish that is compressed with the suffering she has endured from the rape to create the overall experience of *han* which encompasses the inability to express pain, feelings of invisibility, isolation, shame, and self-blame.

Inexpressibility of pain

The inability to describe or communicate one's pain makes it all the more unbearable. Although most would acknowledge experiencing suffering or knowing others who have suffered, clear explanations of suffering are consistently elusive. Virginia Woolf states, "The merest schoolgirl, when she falls in love, has Shakespeare or Keats to speak her mind for her; but let a sufferer try to describe a pain in his head to a doctor and language at once runs dry."[35]

According to Elaine Scarry, "whatever pain achieves, it achieves in part through its unsharability, and it ensures this unsharability through its resistance to language."[36] While victims of rape experience their suffering as a prime reality and often the very focus of their lives, others cannot understand what they are feeling and are part of the larger culture that further victimizes women. Although one can be aware that another person is suffering, she is unaware of what causes that suffering or what that specific experience of suffering is. In this way, suffering also involves the experience of isolation. Consequently, the suffering is heightened by this intrinsic loneliness. Eric Cassel explains,

> Because the sufferer's loss of connection with the group is one of the most important aspects of suffering both from the standpoint of its origins and its opportunities for relief, the loneliness of the sufferer is not only the feeling of being alone but an absence from the general "we-ness" of the world, from a shared participation of the spirit.[37]

Thus, suffering is inexpressible and the inability to communicate suffering results in disconnection and isolation, thereby intensifying the anguish of the victim.

Feelings of isolation as a result of suffering were described through the testimony of multiple women in Chapter 3. Susan described being unable to discuss her suffering, wanting to keep her reality a secret, and feeling that she was living in an "alien world." According to Nancy, her pain was so deep and isolating that she wished she had physical wounds that could actually be tended to. Debbie stated that she felt completely isolated in her abusive situation and could tell no one of her suffering, stating that it was impossible to describe, particularly because her rapist was her husband. Both Theresa and Lori described feeling zombie-like and unable to express their pain; Theresa specifically recounted feeling completely isolated by her suffering and unable to reach out to anyone.

Invisibility

Due to social notions about rape and the community's reaction to the victim, women feel invisible. Societal response acts to de-socialize and de-personalize victims of rape, causing the experience of an overall estrangement from the community. Abandonment and isolation are experienced as a result and the victim is "cast out of the human and divine systems of care and protection that sustain life."[38] Subsequently, every relationship is pervaded by a sense of alienation and disconnection. The rape symbolizes an assault on every valuable connection between the victim and the community. The feeling of being betrayed, loss of trust, and recognition of the potential for harm severely rupture communal ties and erode every facet of relational life for the victim. "When trust is lost, traumatized people feel that they belong more to the dead than to the living."[39]

This is well demonstrated by both Susan and Nancy, who described feeling that their lives had ended during their rapes. Susan stated that she questioned whether she had died during her assault and that the line between life and death had become blurred. In addition, her wanting to keep her rape a secret and her loved ones' denial about her assault contributed to her feelings of disconnect. Nancy explained that following the rape she felt as if she were dying and no longer recognized her life as her own. Also, she quickly realized that if she tried to discuss her rape with anyone other than police or counselors she was immediately shut down and treated as if her rape were an embarrassing, shameful, and inappropriate topic to discuss.[40]

Jan and I. both offered testimony that described experiences of rejection by their communities. Jan was told by her pastor that she was no longer an appropriate candidate to join the sisterhood of the Catholic Church because she had been raped. I. stated that being raped was very shameful and explained that, because of her assault, no man would want to marry her. Likewise, Katie and Angela both felt that the military participated in their assaults and each felt a major disconnect from the community they once called home. Angela stated that she felt completely betrayed by the military and that this betrayal and the reaction of her community after the rape were far worse than the assault itself. Lori felt such a disconnect from her community that shortly after her rape she moved to a different state.[41]

Dr. Shazia, Mukhtar, "Qatif Girl," and Anita all described not only feelings of disconnect from their communities, but being further assaulted by society. Dr. Shazia's grandfather-in-law called her a stain on the family honor and demanded that his grandson divorce her. Mukhtar stated that women in her situation are urged to commit suicide, it being the only means to preserve family honor. "Qatif Girl"'s brother attempted to murder her because she was raped. Anita explained that her community rejected her following her return home after being trafficked. She stated that she was not allowed to see her children and that her husband no longer wanted her. She felt completely alone.

Shame and self-blame

Shame, a poisonous result of the suffering women endured during and following a rape, is defined by the Oxford English Dictionary as "the painful emotion arising from the consciousness of something dishonoring, ridiculous, or indecorous in one's own conduct of circumstances, or of being in a situation which offends one's sense of modesty or decency."[42] This definition supports the societal view that the victim has acted in a way that has brought her shame. After being brutally violated and abused, women feel powerless, humiliated, and ashamed. Although they have done nothing wrong, society's response to their victimization tells them something different. According to Park, "In spite of the fact that a rape victim needs privacy, human dignity, and security, the media exposes every aspect of her life so that there is no place to hide."[43] While many victims of rape choose not to report for the very reasons Park states, they nevertheless experience the second assault of society's response through their own awareness and understanding of the community's perception of women who have suffered sexual violence. As Brené Brown explains, women experience shame as

> the intensely painful feeling or experience of believing we are flawed and therefore unworthy of acceptance and belonging. Women often experience shame when they are entangled in a web of layered, conflicting and competing social-community expectations. Shame leaves women feeling trapped, powerless and isolated.[44]

Shame, which is invariably aimed inward, has the invasive ability to subsume parts of the victim's identity. While shame is initiated by the assault, it works its way into the consciousness and becomes rooted in the perception of self. According to Kathryn Quina and Nancy Carlson, who emphasize shame as a significant element in the experience of rape, the feeling of being dirty following the assault incorporates major segments of the woman's self-concept. The victim may see herself as soiled, damaged, and immoral, with the rape leaving her full of self-hatred and repulsed by her body.[45]

Shame invoked by sexual violence often merges with cultural and religious views of woman as temptress or defiled. Women are denigrated as being unclean during menstruation and are claimed to beguile men with their sexuality.

The shame and self-blame that result from rape are nurtured by these deeply embedded cultural myths. As West explains,

> Women's open expression of sexuality is already sullied by its common linkage to immodest or whorish behavior in popular cultural definitions of femininity. Especially when she is raped by an acquaintance, a "date," or a spouse, a woman can easily equate any sexual interest or attraction she may have felt prior to the incident with the behavior of "scummy" bad girls.[46]

Shame and self-blame relate to each other in a cyclical fashion, with one causing the other and vice versa. Questions of why the victim was chosen to be raped by the perpetrator often surface. She may think that she caused the assault in some way, which is reinforced by stereotypes that are perpetuated in rape culture. Women are labeled as "asking for it" because of their clothing, sexual history, alcohol consumption, and so on. Being female is viewed as "exuding sexual signals that invite exploitation by men."[47] The idea that women "naturally" provoke men into committing "justifiable" rape results from these characterizations. "Self-blame" is often wrapped in a discrediting, slippery package called "the authentic victim." Based on some idea of what constitutes an "authentic" rape experience, women often grapple with a sense of personal failure or self-doubt which can fuel their sense of shame.[48]

Feelings of shame and self-blame can be amplified by androcentric Christian traditions and teachings that deem women's sexuality as sinful, particularly for victims who turn to faith as a resource. The well-known myth of the Fall and other biblical stories such as the tales of Delilah and Jezebel depict women as temptresses, encouraging presumptions about women that support notions of rape victims deserving blame. In addition, teachings that emphasize virginity and condemn sexual acts outside of marriage promote the perception of sin committed by the victim. The idea of women's uncleanliness functions to subjugate women and deny them particular roles. West explains,

> When biblical injunctions about menstruating women or Jesus' cleansing of the hemorrhaging woman are taught in churches, women, unworthiness, illness, and vagina-related "uncleanliness" may all be placed in an interlocked relationship with one another. When these are left as a pile of equatable images, the message that women are somehow fundamentally tainted is communicated.[49]

Alienation from God and faith communities as a result of shame is encouraged by these teachings and practices.

Feelings of shame and self-blame are constant themes in both the stories of women found in various religious texts and contexts (see Chapter 2) and women's contemporary testimonies (see Chapter 3). Regardless of the type of rape endured, culture, religion, social status, or other qualifying factors, in

Chapter 3 each woman described feelings of shame and/or self-blame within her testimony. Multiple women described feelings of wanting to die and some stated that they attempted suicide as a result of the extreme shame they felt.

Susan, Dr. Shazia, Nancy, and Andrea each experienced stranger rape, a type of rape that is generally accepted by society to be no fault of the victim. Yet, each of them still described feelings of shame and self-blame. Susan stated, "in spite of my conviction that I had done nothing wrong, I felt ashamed."[50] Dr. Shazia stated that she had been called kari, meaning that she had stained her family's honor, and thought that she should commit suicide. Nancy blamed herself, repeatedly questioning why she had not fought harder and why she had "caved to his demands," asking if she was a "despicable coward."[51] Andrea said that, had she known the suffering she would endure following the rape, "I would have tried to overdose."[52]

Robin, who was date-raped, stated that she was unable to acknowledge she had been raped until her rapist admitted that he had indeed raped her. In spite of the fact that her rapist had used a knife to subdue her, Robin had questioned how she could have been raped if she had known and had consented to sex with her rapist before. Following his admission, Robin stated, "When I finally calmed down, there was still anger. But most of it was anger at myself."[53] Likewise, Debbie was unable to use the word "rape" to describe the assaults she endured. She felt degraded and judged by others, saying, "It was like I had no right to press charges."[54]

Lori, Rachel, and Ruth, who were also date-raped, described questioning themselves and having feelings of being at fault for their assaults. Lori stated, "I thought it was my fault. What did I do to make him think he could do something like that? Was I wrong in kissing him? Was I wrong to go out with him, to go over his house?"[55] According to Rachel, she immediately felt ashamed, stating, "I felt dirty, violated. I thought it was my fault. It wasn't like he did something to me, it was like I let him do something to me, so I felt very bad about myself."[56] Ruth stated that she was "hopelessly naive" and should never have gone with her rapist; she felt she should have known better.[57]

Kayla, Sally, Karen, and Debbie all experienced spousal or marital rape and all discussed feelings of shame. Kayla stated that, following the rapes, she felt dirty and needed to shower to clean herself. In addition, she stated that she would pretend that nothing had happened in order to protect herself from the pain she felt. Likewise, Sally discussed feeling the need to clean herself following her rapes, stating, "I went into the shower and I washed myself and scrubbed myself. I did everything a rape victim would do. Everything. It was like you knew what had been done to you and that this was something all rape victims do."[58] Karen described feeling ashamed and disgusted; she also vomited following her rape. Debbie was unable to tell anyone about her repeated assaults because of the shame she felt due to the fact that it was her husband who was raping her.

Amy and "Qatif Girl" both experienced gang rape. The assaults occurred in very different cultures and circumstances, yet each woman described similar feelings of shame and self-blame. Amy, who was "gang-banged" at a fraternity party, stated that she felt at fault for her assault: "I felt real stupid about being in such a vulnerable position. I was very angry at myself for getting drunk. This made me feel that I was somewhat responsible."[59] "Qatif Girl," who was kidnapped and gang-raped by seven men, stated that she had shamed her family, and she was further assaulted when her brother tried to kill her as a way to preserve the family honor. She described feeling such shame and humiliation that she attempted suicide twice.

Mukhtar was gang-raped by men of a tribe of higher prestige as a way to shame her family and experienced what has been designated "honor rape." The entire purpose of this rape is to shame the victim and her family. Mukhtar stated, "I feel guilty for having been raped."[60] She described feeling such incredible shame that she believed her only recourse was to drink acid and commit suicide; she felt that she was "dead in the eyes of others."[61] Mukhtar explained, "that is what women do in my situation."[62]

B., Jan, I., and Honorata, also from different cultures, religious backgrounds, social strata, etc., each experienced rape in the context of war. These women were brutalized as a military tactic, yet they still suffered feelings of shame. B. described feeling ashamed and wanting to die after being repeatedly gang-raped alongside other women. Jan described her rape as "worse than dying." She stated that, following her rape, she tried to scrub away the shame she felt: "feeling that if only I would wash everything away from my body it would be all right."[63] In addition, Jan's shame was amplified when she was told by a priest that she could not be a nun, due to her rape. She questioned herself, asking, "Was I not good enough now to embrace the religious life? Had I suddenly changed? Was I soiled and dirty?"[64] I. explained that she experienced great shame as a result of her rape and that no one would marry her. She stated, "No one will want me. It is very shameful."[65] She stated that once she was reunited with her children she was ashamed of what had happened to her: "I avoided people, I shut myself away and it was terrible."[66]

Rebekah, Katie, and Angela, who were raped in the military, struggled with feelings of shame. Rebekah stated that she was re-traumatized by the investigation process and felt shamed by the chaplain, who told her that "God was trying to get my attention."[67] Angela described feeling ashamed and betrayed by the military. She stated that she felt her reputation was sacrificed and that she was "hung out to dry."[68] Katie stated that she was ashamed and humiliated. The military's lack of assistance, victim blaming attitude, and poor treatment of her, as well as the fact that her mother blamed her for the attack, all contributed to her feelings of shame.

Anita and Theresa, both victims of trafficking, experienced their brutal assaults in very different cultures. Anita, who had been kidnapped and forced into trafficking, suffered multiple beatings before submitting to prostitution because of the extreme shame that accompanied it. She stated that once she had finally escaped and returned home, she was scorned by her community. Her children were taken from her and she is not allowed to see them because she has been raped. Although proud of the fact that she helped other women to escape from the brothel, she still felt ashamed because of what happened to her. Theresa, who was trafficked by men in her neighborhood while living under her parents' roof, recounted feeling incredible shame and blaming herself for her repeated rapes.[69]

Conclusion

Twenty-five different women, twenty-five different cases of rape, from different geographical locations, cultures, religious backgrounds, social strata, etc., and all the victims experienced shame and/or self-blame as a result of their attacks. Looking back over each of these women's testimonies and the construction of *han* for rape victims makes it clear that each of these women suffered an intense *han* that wounded her spirit.

For victims of rape, the brutal attack itself, followed by the community response of a rape culture, results in the experience of *han* which causes the core of a woman's nature, her embodiment of the divine, to be broken. The victim's perception of self is altered, which ultimately begets a spiritual death. The rape itself takes away the woman's ability to control her own body and wounds the personal self. The societal response of blaming the victim creates shame that becomes rooted in the perception of self, causing her to view herself as "dirty" and immoral, no longer capable of embodying the divine.

It would be inappropriate to conclude that the women whose testimony has been offered experienced a spiritual death. To do so would be to victimize and would contribute to the overall culture that seeks to leave women powerless. Whether or not a spiritual death has occurred can be determined only by the women themselves. However, what can be concluded from the testimony presented is that each woman suffered not only as a result of her rape but also because of the prevailing rape culture, which influenced society's general reaction towards her and contributed to her own reaction towards herself. This suffering can be identified as *han*, and this *han* wounds the spirit. As any untended wound results in the risk of death, the continued suffering of *han* without treatment can result in the risk of spiritual death.

However, although a spiritual death may occur, this is not a permanent reality; rather, it is a temporary state that can be overcome. The opportunity to make it so and achieve a spiritual resurrection will be discussed in the following chapter.

Notes

1 Judith Lewis Herman, *Trauma and Recovery* (New York: Basic Books, 1992), p. 52.
2 Following Beverly Lanzetta's definition (p. 28), I understand mystical as referring "not only to personal experience, but also to the principles and processes of the inner life, including prayer, spiritual direction, techniques of contemplation, languages of the sacred, images of the divine, and the commitment of the individual to a process of spiritual growth and transformation."

3 Ibid.
4 Ewert Cousins, preface to the series *World Spirituality: An Encyclopedic History of the Religious Quest*. Vol. 1 (New York: Crossroad, 1987), p. xiii.
5 Sandra M. Schneiders, "Spirituality in the Academy," in Bradley Hanson, ed., *Modern Christian Spirituality: Methodological and Historical Essays* (Atlanta: Scholars Press, 1990), p. 17.
6 Ibid.
7 Lanzetta, p. 29.
8 Rita Nakashima Brock, *Journeys by Heart: A Christology of Erotic Power* (New York: Crossroad, 1988), p. 13.
9 Noddings, p. 40.
10 Mary Daly, *Pure Lust: Elemental Feminist Philosophy* (Boston: Beacon Press, 1984), p. 58. Daly adds in a footnote that religious asceticism practiced by females is not an exclusive Christian practice.
11 Ruether, p. 169.
12 Mary Daly, *Beyond God the Father* (Boston: Beacon Press, 1973), p. 77.
13 Carol J. Adams, "'I Just Raped My Wife! What Are You Going to do about it, Pastor?' The Church and Sexual Violence," in Buchwald *et al.*, eds., p. 69.
14 Ibid., p. 70.
15 Note that victims who maintain belief systems that do not uphold the existence of a divine being ultimately experience a loss of self in relation to a larger power, which affects their overall existence and results in a "spiritual death." The larger power will be determined by the belief system.
16 Andrew Sung Park, "Sin," in Miguel A. De La Torre, ed., *Handbook of US Theologies of Liberation* (St. Louis: Chalice Press, 2004), p. 115.
17 Suh Nam-Dong, "Towards a Theology of Han," in Minjung Theology (Singapore: CCA, 1981), p. 65, quoted in Chung Hyun Kyung, "*Han-Pu-Ri*: Doing Theology from Korean Women's Perspective." *The Ecumenical Review* 40(1) (January 1988): pp. 25–36, 30.
18 Hyun Young-Hak, "Minjung the Suffering Servant and Hope." Lecture given at James Memorial Chapel, Union Theological Seminary, New York, April 13, 1982, p. 7, quoted in Chung Hyun Kyung, p. 30.
19 Andrew Sung Park, *Racial Conflict and Healing: An Asian-American Theological Perspective* (Maryknoll: Orbis Books, 1996), p. 9.
20 See Dorothee Sölle, *Suffering* (Philadelphia: Fortress Press, 1975).
21 Chung Hyun Kyung, *Struggle to Be the Sun Again: Introducing Asian Women's Theology* (Maryknoll: Orbis Books, 1990), p. 42.
22 Ibid.
23 See Park, *Racial Conflict and Healing* and *The Wounded Heart of God: The Asian Concept of* Han *and the Christian Doctrine of Sin*. Nashville: Abingdon Press, 1993.
24 Park, *Racial Conflict and Healing*, p. 9.
25 See Carl Jung, *Letters*. ed. G. Adler (Princeton: Princeton University Press, 1973).
26 Park, *The Wounded Heart of God*, p. 33.
27 Ibid., p. 34.
28 Park, *From Hurt to Healing*, p. 15.
29 Vanessa Veselka, "The Collapsible Woman: Cultural Response to Rape and Sexual Abuse," in Lisa Jervis and Andi Zeisler, eds., *Bitchfest* (New York: Farrar, Straus and Giroux, 2006), p. 57.
30 Livy, Ab urbe condita, 2:58, quoted in Donaldson, p. 22.
31 See Young, pp. 279–286.
32 Pope Pius XII, quoted in Young, p. 282.
33 Mary Pellauer, "A Theological Perpective on Sexual Assault," in Mary D. Pellauer, Barbara Chester, and Jane A. Boyajian, eds., *Sexual Assault and Abuse:*

A Handbook for Clergy and Religious Professionals (San Francisco: Harper & Row, 1987), p. 84.
34 West, p. 12.
35 Virginia Woolf, "On Being Ill," in *The Moment and Other Essays* (New York: Harcourt Brace Jovanovich, 1948), p. 11, quoted in Elaine Scarry, *The Body in Pain: The Making and Unmaking of the World* (New York: Oxford University Press, 1985), p. 4.
36 Ibid.
37 Eric Cassel, "Pain and Suffering," in Warren Thomas Reich, ed., *Encyclopedia of Bioethics*. Vol. 4, rev. edn. (New York: Macmillan Library Reference USA/Simon & Schuster Macmillan, 1995), p. 1902, quoted in Kristine M. Rankka, *Women and the Value of Suffering: An Aw(e)ful Rowing Toward God* (Collegeville: Liturgical Press, 1998), pp. 16–17.
38 Herman, p. 52.
39 Ibid.
40 See Raine, p. 43.
41 See Warshaw, p. 17.
42 *Oxford English Dictionary*. 2nd edn. (Oxford: Oxford University Press, 1989).
43 Park, *From Hurt to Healing*, pp. 40–41.
44 Brené Brown, *Women and Shame* (Austin: 3C Press, 2004), p. 30.
45 Kathryn Quina and Nancy Carlson, *Rape, Incest, and Sexual Harassment: A Guide for Helping Survivors* (New York: Greenwood Press, 1989), p. 30.
46 West, p. 69.
47 Ibid., p. 71.
48 Ibid.
49 Ibid., p. 75.
50 Brison, p. 13.
51 Raine, p. 26.
52 Rushing, p. 11.
53 Warshaw, p. 6.
54 Madigan and Gamble, p. 43.
55 Bergen, pp. 16–17.
56 Ibid., p. 30.
57 Pierce-Baker, p. 89.
58 Bergen, p. 33.
59 Sanday, *Fraternity Gang Rape*, p. 101.
60 Mai, p. 23.
61 Ibid., p. 19.
62 Ibid., p. 18.
63 Ruff-O'Herne, p. 75.
64 Ibid., p. 127.
65 Goodwin.
66 UNIFEM.
67 "Hearing Testimony of Rebekah Havrilla before the Military Personnel Subcommittee of the Senate Armed Services Committee."
68 Hope and Eriksen.
69 Flores, pp. 48–51.

6 Spiritual resurrection
Han-Pu-Ri and momentary salvation

> Victims need to name their world, so that the terror and violence will stop, and so that they will no longer be victimized but will become survivors.
>
> Carol Adams[1]

Paths for healing are presented in many forms; however, those that are based in patriarchal tradition are problematic and can fail victims of sexual assault. While Christianity, and other patriarchal traditions, should not be dismissed as irredeemably oppressive, methods of empowerment found in Christian discourse, twelve-step groups, and other paths that have patriarchal foundations are problematic and call for women to remain passive, submissive victims. Jennifer Manlowe explains,

> As a woman, a survivor has been taught, in a multitude of ways, to hang her security upon external validation. Female redemption is to come from outside herself – from the approval of others, from a male savior, or in a twelve-step parlance, from a Higher Power.[2]

However, a part of the empowerment process for a rape victim is disentangling these messages and their meanings, as they lead only to "repeating the paradigm of helpless victim."[3] Affirming relationships that do not demand one to be obedient and surrender are needed in order to begin the healing process and to achieve a spiritual resurrection.

There is no doubt that a reinterpretation of Christian teachings, as well as other patriarchal religious traditions, is necessary in order to lessen the wounding of the woman's spirit and support healing.[4] This said, the goal of what follows is not to continue a discussion on patriarchal traditions, but rather to explore a path for healing and spiritual resurrection that breaks away from traditional theological thought.

The healing of one's self-image and ridding oneself of *han* are the first steps towards healing and salvation. These opportunities exist within our daily lives and can be achieved through the practice of *Han-Pu-Ri*, a shamanistic ritual which is carried out to release the *han* of one person or a collective population. The following will define spiritual resurrection, examine the practice of

Han-Pu-Ri, and demonstrate how this practice offers healing for victims of sexual violence that is not limited by patriarchal structure and allows them to transform from victim to survivor.

Spiritual resurrection

As discussed, the continued suffering resulting from experiencing sexual violence, a re-victimization by the rape culture, and the inability to express pain as well as invisibility and feelings of shame and blame that lead to the loss of self-worth and construct the victim's *han* can ultimately bring about a spiritual death. Whereas traditional Christian theology claims a male savior redeems us through his death and resurrection, Brock explains that

> no one heroic or divine deed will defeat oppressive powers and death-delivering systems. We cannot rely on one past event to save the future. No almighty power will deliver us from evil. With each minute we wait for a rescue, more die.[5]

Rather, life-giving powers are offered by community and our ability to speak our truth, to be heard, and to create change in an unjust system. Thus, in order to achieve a spiritual resurrection, the victim must release her *han* and heal her self-image with the support of her community. This can be achieved through the shamanistic practice of *Han-Pu-Ri*.

Han-Pu-Ri

Han-Pu-Ri, the untangling of the complex web of *han* through "survival wisdom," arose from Korean shamanistic tradition and offers ghosts who are voiceless the opportunity to speak about their experience of *han*. This ritual calls for the community to be accountable and release the *han* either by eliminating oppression or by comforting the ghosts. It can be practiced gently through song, dance, and ritual or militantly through organized political movements. *Han-Pu-Ri* can be an opportunity for collective healing and spiritual resurrection for *han*-ridden spirits as well as for collective repentance for the communities that have participated in creating and perpetuating *han*.

In Korean shamanistic tradition, the ritual of *Han-Pu-Ri* offers women the opportunity to become active agents of liberation. It is performed primarily by women priestesses, and women are both the majority of those who participate in the ritual of *Han-Pu-Ri* and those whose ghost stories are told. According to Chung Hyun Kyung, "These factors provide an important clue for the hermeneutics of suspicion." In asking, "Why are women the majority in the above situation," Chung states that the answer is clear: "Korean women have been the embodiment of the worst *Han* of our (Korean) history."[6] Because women often do not have the public channels to communicate the *han* they are experiencing, a sense of impassibility or "living death" is developed. This shared experience among women allows them to understand one another, and *Han-Pu-Ri* has become a space where Korean women are not dominated by patriarchal religious authorities and can play a spiritual role. *Han-Pu-Ri* offers Korean women the opportunity to come together and release their *han*.

Han-Pu-Ri is comprised of three important steps: speaking and hearing, naming, and changing. In speaking and hearing, the shaman provides the persons or ghosts with the opportunity to break their silence, express their *han*, and be heard by the community. The second step, naming, allows the source of oppression to be identified by the persons or ghosts. Finally, changing is the attainment of peace by the persons or ghosts through the transforming of unjust situations through action.

Korean women practice *Han-Pu-Ri* in gentle ways by expressing suffering and resistance through song, proverbs, and folklore; using humor and satire, they are enabled to move beyond "paralyzing sadness."[7] Referencing Lee Oo Chung, Chung Hyun Kyung states, "Through folktales and songs Korean women have satirized the greed of political authorities, the foolishness of aristocrats and intellectuals, the hypocrisy of male priests and their religious institutions, and the brutality of the patriarchal family."[8]

Unlike Christian theological teaching and Western culture in general, these "gentle ways" do not celebrate "heroic despair" or engage dualistic thinking related to body and spirit or physical and spiritual realms. Women who practice *Han-Pu-Ri* in this manner emphasize what Lee calls "present centered optimism"; they believe that by coming together to endure and challenge *han*, they will triumph in this lifetime. The positive relationship with labor, as highlighted by Korean folk arts, celebrates harmony between life and nature and the honoring of love of neighbor encourages wisdom rather than violence as the means of overcoming evil.

Militant resistance has also become a primary way of practicing *Han-Pu-Ri* in recent times, with movements predominantly led by women. Movements in Korea and other Asian nations that are challenging patriarchal society are on the rise. Chung explains,

> There are the movements against dowry and sati in India; the movements against military dictatorships, multinational corporations, and the international prostitution industry in the Philippines; the ecological movement in Japan; and the movement against state terrorism in Sri Lanka. Asian women have discovered their true selves and have become stronger through their participation in these movements.[9]

Through these acts, women are breaking their silence, naming their *han*, and confronting the larger systems that have perpetrated their oppression; in doing so, transformation is made possible.

A theological methodology has been developed by the Korean Association of Women Theologians (KAWT) in order to lessen the suffering of women and employ steps that are similar to the shamanistic *Han-Pu-Ri*. Listening to the *han*-ridden testimonies of women was the starting point of their theologizing. The second step consisted of the women theologians teaming up with social scientists and other women who were familiar with structural elements of the problems in order to perform a social analysis. Following this analysis, focusing on questions raised through the two previous steps, they offered theological reflections, sharing them with the women who offered their testimony and the community in order to inquire whether or not the articulated theology was empowering to them. In the final step, KAWT participated in protests and demonstrations in order to work to heal the *han* of women.

Through this methodology, KAWT has correctly identified women's lived experience as the most crucial source for doing women's theology in addition to critical consciousness and tradition as important resources for fully articulating this theology. As Chung explains,

> The specific historical experience of Korean women is manifested in their experience as victims and agents of liberation, and through the experience of *han* and *Han-Pu-Ri*. Korean women's experience is the starting point and ending point of Korean women's hermeneutical circle.[10]

Han-Pu-Ri *and sexual violence: from victim to survivor*

Han-Pu-Ri, or "women's process of hearing into speech,"[11] is an important resource for women who have experienced sexual violence. This traditional ritual practiced by Korean women is applicable to rape victims because women who have been sexually assaulted have also experienced what can be characterized as the worst *han* in women's history. Society has made that clear through its continual message that no worse thing can occur in a female's life than being raped. Like the Korean women who practice *Han-Pu-Ri*, rape victims also have no channel to express their *han*, which leads to a sense of isolation and impassibility or "living death." However, women who have been sexually assaulted can begin healing through speaking out, naming the wrong committed against them, and calling for the community to hear their voices and be accountable for its injustice. Coming together with others to share their stories, speak their pain, and experience a sense of accompaniment will begin the process of releasing their *han* and begin the spiritual resurrection process.

The practice of *Han-Pu-Ri* for victims of sexual violence can occur through both gentle and militant ways. Central in these efforts are rape crisis centers (RCC), which have been established as feminist organizations with the purpose of emphasizing the advancement and nurturance of women. These centers were founded as non-bureaucratic, non-hierarchical, collectivist organizations that are free of elitism. They therefore break away from the patriarchal culture of the greater community and create an environment that focuses on women's experience and empowers women to break their silence.

RCCs are recognized for establishing strategies to begin the healing process for victims of sexual violence. For instance, "Take Back the Night" has become a means of allowing rape victims to achieve the steps of *Han-Pu-Ri*. This event is organized to protest rape culture and the oppression of women and typically consists of speak-outs, rallies, marches, and candlelit vigils that take a stand against violence against women. The Take Back the Night event provides a public forum for victims of sexual assault, as well as all women and men who are victimized by the current rape culture, to voice how they have been wronged and denounce the unjust patriarchal system, and for the community to hear the injustice, resulting in a transformation. Although some may claim that Take Back the Night is no more than group therapy, it offers a spiritual encounter through an end to isolation, empowerment, and sense of accompaniment within a community of women who share a similar experience.

More recently, SlutWalks[12] have become a transnational movement to challenge the rape culture. Beginning in Toronto in 2011 in response to comments made by Constable Michael Sanguinetti, who suggested that women should not dress like "sluts" if they don't want to be raped, rallies have been organized around the world in which women dress "slutty" and march through the streets. They are often organized by sexual assault survivors and include "speak-outs," where women share their experiences of rape with the community. Although controversial, SlutWalks confront the culture and offer voice to those who have experienced sexual violence. Like Take Back the Night, this movement offers the opportunity to achieve *Han-Pu-Ri* and allows the healing process to begin.

While Take Back the Night and SlutWalks offer the practice of *Han-Pu-Ri* on a large scale, not every woman will find that these movements are the right place to begin her spiritual resurrection process. Women can participate in *Han-Pu-Ri* on any scale. Community can be two people. By reaching out to one other individual, the rape victim can accomplish the steps and begin her journey of spiritual resurrection. As Brock notes, "the community sustains life-giving power by its memory of its own brokenheartedness and of those who have suffered and gone before and by its members being courageously and redemptively present."[13] Because the divine is experienced within those intimate interactions with others, the woman is able to achieve salvation.

If a spiritual resurrection is to occur, silence must be broken. Brock and Thistlethwaite explain,

> silence is death. Breaking silence is a movement of grace. It shatters the pain and denial that squeezes the breath out of us. It opens doors for the new breezes of life, hope, and liberating action. Always tell, and always tell with friends to help you remember.[14]

It is through these rituals, which are led by women, that safe space is created, *han* can be spoken, and listening and solidarity are commanded. Rape culture and its injustice are challenged.

A spiritual resurrection can occur following the ritual of *Han-Pu-Ri*, allowing the victim to transform into survivor. This permits the woman to reclaim her body, and thus her self-image. In doing so, the now survivor is able to claim her anger. According to Brock, this anger is freeing and must be "recognized and embraced as an aspect of ourselves."[15] It is an important tool that allows women to understand their pain and determine what is acceptable for their wellbeing. She explains that

> Buried anger is closely tied to the body because the body is the home of the heart. Bodies are our first, closest, and most powerful connection to both ourselves and all else ... Through our experiences of pain and humiliation, we learn to control and ignore the body; and any embodied contact with the world becomes ambivalent. The false self learns to ... hate the body, turning anger inward. Reclamation of the body is part of the reclamation of self as awareness of physical pain and stress can become important clues to psychic and spiritual distress.[16]

Although the release of *han*, embracing anger, reclaiming the body, and healing of the self-image allow for a spiritual resurrection, we must note that such a resurrection is a process that is achieved through daily experiences. As Gebara asserts, they will be momentary resurrections rather than a permanent state that one achieves.

> It [resurrection] is there like a glass of water that quenches thirst for the moment, but thirst comes again, sometimes stronger than before ... The moment of the hoped for salvation comes, sometimes seen, sometimes unforeseen ... This fragile redemption is what we find in the everyday life of every person. Today it is the story of the life and speech of women.[17]

Although *han* has been released, healing has begun, and spiritual resurrection has occurred, suffering will not simply cease to exist. Salvation is not separate from suffering; rather, they are intertwined. The brutal assault permanently altered the existence and psyche of the woman and is one that will be carried with her throughout her life. In addition, the rape culture continues to exist and continues to cause pain and destruction. Thus, momentary resurrections are necessary to quell her continued spiritual affliction.

Han-Pu-Ri *in practice*

Kwon In-Sook, a labor activist who had been expelled from her university for involvement with a student movement, was arrested for being a subversive in the summer of 1986 in Korea. She was beaten and sexually tortured by a police detective for refusing to reveal the names of accomplices. The brutal and devastating assault left Ms Kwon feeling ashamed, humiliated, and wanting to commit suicide, as was called for by the traditional Confucian culture. Although she suffered greatly and at times thought taking her own life was the only way to end the torment she endured, Ms Kwon found strength through her liberationist consciousness and shared her experience with her community. She wrote a letter demanding that her torturer be arrested and held accountable for her assault. While her request was not taken seriously and was discarded by the chief of security, news traveled of her demand; women prisoners jailed alongside her went on hunger strike and stood in solidarity with her. The following day, the male prisoners joined the hunger strike.[18]

Ms Kwon was the first woman to speak out about sexual violence in Korean history. Sexual torture had been a common practice; however, the victims had never spoken out for fear of being further brutalized or endangering their families. Nevertheless, Ms Kwon found her voice and broke the culture of silence. In doing so, she spoke her *han*. The community listened to Ms Kwon's voice and stood with her in solidarity, creating change in the overall culture of silence. Ms Kwon's story embodies the essence of *Han-Pu-Ri*.

As Ms Kwon put *Han-Pu-Ri* into practice, releasing her *han*, so did each of the women whose testimony was presented in Chapter 3. Twenty-five women courageously shared their stories of trauma, suffering, and *han*. They voiced their experiences for the world to hear in hopes that sharing their realities would prompt change and permeate the prevalent rape culture. While some women stopped short of describing their overall healing process, others offered further details that recounted their experiences of releasing *han*. Here, the stories of Nancy and Mukhtar will be continued. These women are from different cultures and religious backgrounds and each pursued healing in a different way. Their personal experiences of practicing *Han-Pu-Ri*, releasing *han*, and achieving survivorship are described below.

Nancy

Nancy's experience of rape, her interaction with police and medical staff following her assault, and the reaction of her loved ones constructed an unbearable *han*. She described feeling that she was dying and that her life was no longer her own. This being said, Nancy participated in the practice of *Han-Pu-Ri* and released her *han* in several steps. She began by working with a counselor who helped her to draft letters to family and friends who had belittled her experience or refused to allow her to voice her *han*. In doing so, where Nancy was once denied, she was now granted the opportunity to speak her *han* and voiced the injustices perpetrated against her both by her rapist and by the community, challenging the overarching social structure of rape culture in the process.

In addition to confronting the rape culture, Nancy experienced community outside of the counseling office. Reuniting with her old friend Victoria, Nancy found not only companionship but also the realization that she was not alone in her suffering. Victoria had previously disclosed to Nancy that she too had been raped and had told no one because of her feelings of shame.

Upon learning of Nancy's assault, Victoria came to see her and listened to her voice her *han*. Nancy stated,

> I told her my story. She did not offer advice. She did not pretend to have a map in her hip pocket. Knowing her story made the telling of mine feel like an exchange rather than a confession. We shared an exile, not an island. She was on her own island, a different shore. She saw me – as I was – and that was the comfort.[19]

Victoria's friendship gave Nancy hope. Following that day, she and Victoria kept in close contact. Nancy would contact Victoria during her "blackest hours," stating that she was able to confide in her "because I knew her own rape made her incapable of judging me."[20] Nancy explained, "And [Victoria's] life was evidence that grace and humor were still possible. Her existence itself was a promise."[21] Thus, for Nancy, having a companion in her life that she could confide in without fear of being belittled, questioned, or told what she should or should not do gave her the opportunity to speak her *han*, know that it had been heard, and focus on her healing process.

Mukhtar

Mukhtar's gang rape as a means of shaming her family left her with a crippling *han* that nearly ended her physical life. As she explained, women who are raped in her culture are called upon to commit suicide in order to preserve family honor. Nevertheless, Mukhtar engaged in *Han-Pu-Ri*, demanding justice and speaking out against the culture that victimized her. In doing so, she garnered international attention. The world listened to Mukhtar's *han* and there was a global outcry for justice on her behalf.

Her demand for justice resulted in her rapists being tried, Mukhtar testifying against them, and each receiving the death penalty. Mukhtar was given police protection and the equivalent of $8,300 by President Pervez Musharraf as victim compensation. Although she had never attended school herself, recognizing that education is pivotal in the process of creating social change, Mukhtar used the money to build two schools in her village, one for girls and one for boys.

In addition to the compensation she received from the Pakistani government, a US aid organization assisted in administering over $100,000 in donations for Mukhtar's efforts, which allowed her to expand the schools she started, found a shelter for abused women, and purchase a van that is utilized as an ambulance in her village. Participating in social change became a crucial part of Mukhtar's healing. Within her community, she has become a lifeline for other women. She is a spokeswoman against rape, honor killing, acid attacks, and other forms of violence against women.

Mukhtar's international attention prompted an invitation to speak to a group of Pakistani-Americans in the United States. However, this attention also angered the dominant culture and resulted in the Pakistani authorities confiscating her passport, placing her under house arrest, and disconnecting her telephone land line. President Musharraf claimed that Mukhtar was "airing her dirty laundry" in full view of the international community and that she was embarrassing Pakistan. Following her detainment, Mukhtar's rapists were released from prison, putting her in great jeopardy.

Although Musharraf attempted to silence Mukhtar once again, she used her cell phone to continue to speak out until the authorities confiscated it and took her into custody. By then, though, her voice had been heard loudly around the globe and the international outcry forced the Pakistani government to relent. Mukhtar was released, her passport and phone were returned, and she was permitted to travel to the US.

Through speaking out against her rapists and the rape culture and not only demanding social change but instigating it, Mukhtar engaged in *Han-Pu-Ri*, releasing her *han* and experiencing survivorship. She has begun her healing process and continues to find salvation in her daily life. Mukhtar is now widely recognized as an advocate for women's human rights and through her humanitarian efforts she experiences multiple momentary resurrections.

Daily resurrections

Although each did so in a different way, both Nancy and Mukhtar participated in the practice of *Han-Pu-Ri* as a means of releasing their *han*, experiencing salvation, and beginning their healing processes. In addition, while their experienced salvations were momentary, they each continued to have daily resurrections through their lived experiences and struggles. Nancy reconnected with community through her counselor and her friend Victoria. This allowed her to speak her *han* and confront those around her who were dismissive and were not giving her the support she needed. Having a friend who had also experienced rape allowed Nancy to recognize that she was not alone in her experience and that shame should not be a part of her suffering. Being able to confide in Victoria without fear of being judged and voicing her suffering allowed Nancy to heal her self-image and experience momentary resurrections.

While Nancy connected to community through her close friend, Mukhtar connected to community by speaking out publicly about the injustices perpetrated against her. The global community's attentiveness and reaction to Mukhtar's *han* allowed her to heal her own self-image and recognize how many other women had suffered similar experiences. Mukhtar's activism and efforts for social change have allowed her to experience momentary resurrections within her daily life.

Both of these women have found salvation through their own courage and willingness to act while remaining fully aware of their vulnerability. It was through their realization that they had the power to liberate themselves, to begin their healing processes, to demand accountability and call for justice by connecting with community that their resurrections were possible. As Brock states, "Our heartfelt action, not alone, but in the fragile, resilient interconnections we share with others, generates the power that makes and sustains life."[22]

Conclusion

The incredible abuse suffered by women who experience sexual violence by their perpetrators and by the larger rape culture is severely wounding; so much so that spiritual death is possible. Although this language may create the image of a permanent state, resurrection *is* possible. If it is appropriate to understand this suffering as *han*, then it is also appropriate to consider *Han-Pu-Ri* as a path to spiritual resurrection.

While traditional Christian theology claims that redemption is possible through the death and resurrection of Christ, as Brock argues,

> The power that gives and sustains life does not flow from a dead and resurrected savior to his followers ... In thinking that a single person, a savior, or even one group can save us, we mistake the crest of a wave for the vast sea churning beneath it.[23]

Rather, the tradition of *Han-Pu-Ri* offers an opportunity for sexual assault victims to speak their *han* within a woman-centered ritual. It is within this community that life-giving power is experienced and resurrection begins. This said, we must also note that resurrection is a state that is "lived and grasped within the confines of our existence."[24] As Gebara explains, resurrection must be identified with salvation and must be linked with the suffering we experience in our lives.

> Salvation will not be something outside the fabric of life but will take place within the heart of it. It springs from the expected and the unexpected, from the near and the far, from the known and the unknown. It can last a short or a long time. It comes and goes, following the swing of life. Salvation has different origins and occurs at different times, intermingled with the confusion of life. Salvation is what helps us live in the present moment, even when it feeds a dream of greater happiness.[25]

Thus, resurrection is not an irreversible state one achieves; rather, resurrection can be found in everyday experiences and has multiple occurrences. It is the experience of "recovering life and hope and justice along life's path even when these experiences are frail and fleeting ... [It is] not a point of arrival but a little oasis in the midst of daily trials."[26] As Gebara affirms, each day must begin in search of resurrection; this task is as crucial for survival as eating or drinking. As our body must be nourished, so must our spirit.

Notes

1 Adams, p. 81.
2 Jennifer L. Manlowe, "Seduced by Faith: Sexual Traumas and Their Embodied Effects," in Adams and Fortune, eds., p. 329.
3 Ibid.
4 For a comprehensive feminist reinterpretation of the Christian tradition, see Brock.
5 Ibid., p. 105.
6 Chung, "*Han-Pu-Ri*: Doing Theology from Korean Women's Perspective," p. 35.
7 Lee Oo Chung, "Korean Traditional Culture and Feminist Theology," in *The Task of Korean Feminist Theology* (Seoul: Korean Association of Women Theologians, 1983), p. 77, cited in Chung, *Struggle to Be the Sun Again*, p. 43.
8 Ibid.
9 Ibid., p. 44.
10 Ibid., p. 36.
11 Rita Nakashima Brock and Susan Brooks Thistlethwaite, *Casting Stones: Prostitution and Liberation in Asia and the United States* (Minneapolis: Fortress Press, 1996), p. 284.
12 For additional information, see http://www.slutwalktoronto.com.
13 Brock, p. 105.
14 Brock and Thistlethwaite, p. 285.
15 Brock, p. 21.
16 Ibid.
17 Gebara, p. 123.
18 See Chung, "*Han-Pu-Ri*: Doing Theology from Korean Women's Perspective," pp. 33–34.
19 Raine, p. 149.
20 Ibid.
21 Ibid.
22 Brock, p. 106.
23 Ibid., p. 105.
24 Gebara, p. 122.
25 Ibid., p. 121.
26 Ibid., pp. 122, 125.

7 Conclusion

Rape as a fate worse than death has long existed, causing women to live in a state of constant fear. Women who have endured sexual violence have endured a suffering so deep that their ability to transcend the self is disrupted and their spirits are wounded. While one's faith is often where solace is sought following victimization, religion is not immune to rape culture. An examination of rape within the context of religion demonstrates the deep roots of this misogynistic and violent culture, as well as the ongoing consequences of its lived reality. Looking to biblical texts, the influence of rape culture is found on multiple levels. The texts themselves are androcentric and their interpretations encourage society to ignore sexual violence as well as the women who have suffered it. In addition, as the most influential text in history on "ideas about the place of women and about the relationships of the sexes,"[1] the Bible's rape texts and other narratives that present women in a negative way serve to promote damaging ideas about women, sexual violence, and victimization. Consequently, there is a strong correlation between biblical "texts of terror,"[2] their interpretations, and rape culture.

Purity legends, the lore of virgin martyrdom, and the Christian tradition's sanctifying of women who have sacrificed their lives in order to protect their purity are also extremely harmful to women and support the overarching rape culture. The stories of Lucretia, Thecla, Maria Goretti, and others have encouraged the association of women's sexuality with virginity and motherhood, whereas morality is associated with sexual shame. The influence of this tradition and its manifestation in modern society are massive. Women who are raped have damaged self-images and society participates in the culture by shaming and blaming the victim, contributing to her suffering. For instance, in some cultures, as I. described in Chapter 3, women who are not virgins are unable to marry and are considered unclean, disgraced, and without honor. Consequently, "virginity tests" have become a common practice on girls in some areas; the hymen is examined and, if not intact, the girl is prosecuted and often sent to prison for several years.[3]

Hymen replacement surgery or "virginity repair" has also become a common procedure, particularly for Muslim women (although non-Muslim women are also victims of "virginity repair"), who are often required to provide certificates of virginity preceding the consummation of their marriage.[4] This procedure is also commonly performed within the sex-trafficking industry, as a woman with an intact hymen is of more value to her traffickers. Within the US, doctors are receiving more requests for this procedure. According to cosmetic surgeon Dr. Pamela Loftus,

> the most common reason we hear [for having hymen replacement surgery] is that they [women] have had a negative comment made by a male sexual partner. Women are made to feel that they are not perfect the way they are and often it's the partner that sets this off.[5]

Sexual violence within the context of religion has functioned to harm women, control their sexuality and support the rape culture. Examining rape texts and purity legends demonstrates the ongoing historical and religious legacy of sexual violence against women and a misogynistic culture that encourages rape as a means to control and dominate women. In addition, analysis of these texts reveals the silencing of rape victims, a continued practice in today's society. This is well demonstrated through the twenty-five cases presented in Chapter 3 and the testimonies offered by contemporary women who have suffered sexual violence. These women consistently reported feeling silenced and shamed by the culture and having damaged self-images as a result of their rapes.

Sexual violence is institutional violence, and the ongoing rape culture within modern-day society is manifested in multiple ways. Sex and violence are intertwined and violence against women is the norm. Men have been socialized to be sexual subjects and women sexual objects. To be masculine means to be dominant, in control, and superior; rape is a means of keeping women in their place and rape myths function to validate these ideas and sanction violence against women. Rapist behavior is legitimized not only through the construct of masculinity but also through patriarchal anthropology which proclaims women as sinful, the cause of sin, and subjugated to men as punishment.[6] Thus, justification for rape and victim blaming easily become parts of the overall culture.

Like biblical rape texts and purity legends, disturbing media ads, video games that challenge the player to rape women into submission, and hymen replacement surgery are all manifestations of this misogynistic culture. Television and film continue to image violence against women as sexy while language about rape downplays the act, excuses the rapist, and condemns the victim. In addition, rape culture influences the legal process and promotes victim blaming behavior among law enforcement officials, causing rape to be viewed as a crime not worth prosecuting.

Society's response to rape is different from its response to any other crime. Victims of car jackings, home invasions, assault, murder, etc. are not judged for the crime committed against them. However, victims of rape are viewed at the very least as sharing in the responsibility of their victimization.

This overwhelming message, which women learn from a very young age, that being raped is the worst thing that can happen in their lives and will occur only because of their own misdeeds, is a major component of the victim's suffering. The testimonies of the twenty-five women in Chapter 3 well demonstrate that the deep anguish they endured resulted from both the rape itself and the overall culture that perpetrated an additional victimization, leaving them feeling ashamed and their self-images tainted. Across cultural, racial, religious, class, and other boundaries, these elements of rape culture and the suffering endured by victims remain the same. Thus, it is this multiplicity of suffering deriving from physical violence and rape culture that constructs the rape victim's *han*, and it is the ongoing experience of this *han* in solitude that can result in a spiritual death.

While the term "spiritual death" may give the impression of a permanent reality, it is not an irreversible state. Instead, a shamanistic ritual primarily practiced by females, *Han-Pu-Ri*, offers the opportunity to experience a spiritual resurrection. Being able to speak one's *han*, have it heard by those who have participated in the injustice, and thus prompt social change allow the victim to reflect critically on her suffering, begin to heal her self-image, and achieve self-awakening. As Chung explains, "Self-awakened/self-affirming women take a stand and change their personal and political relationships."[7] This is well demonstrated by Mukhtar Mai's practicing of *Han-Pu-Ri*. Voicing her pain, demanding justice and becoming an advocate for change altered her relationships, political and personal, in both her local and the global community.

Although *Han-Pu-Ri* offers spiritual resurrection, that which is achieved is momentary. Because rape culture continues to exist, resurrection is not a permanent state; rather, it is one that is experienced in multiplicity; it comes and goes and must be sought out day after day. However, recognizing this does not negate the power of spiritual resurrection. Gebara explains,

> Claiming the dailiness of salvation is not to deny the possibilities opened by a perspective on the beyond of history. We must keep the tension between the historical present, which is our concrete lived experience, and this beyond, which is the object of the tradition of our faith and hope.[8]

Confronting rape culture

Addressing the overall structural issues that allow rape culture to exist and pursuing structural healing are necessary. Transforming a rape culture requires society to demand change and address the many elements discussed throughout this text. Rape must be denounced for what it is, an act of violence. Its justification must be rejected and language about rape must acknowledge the brutality of the crime. The status of marital rape as legal in thirteen countries is absolutely outrageous and is an issue that demands global attention. Until these laws are changed, rape within marriage will be viewed as nothing more than a wifely duty. Media that promotes sexual violence must be not only repudiated but made inaccessible. The fact that "RapeLay" and other sexually violent games can be accessed in seconds on the internet is extremely problematic and encourages the culture of violence against women.

Law enforcements' attitudes toward rape must be addressed and changed. While rapes are, of course, prosecuted and victims' reports are taken seriously at times, the reverse is also true. This is due to the overwhelming culture that encourages the blaming of victims. As discussed in Chapter 4, law enforcement officers are not immune to rape culture and are influenced as easily as other individuals within society. This being said, there are opportunities for addressing this key concern. First, it would be advantageous to train women police officers to take rape reports and work with women who have been sexually violated. In addition, training led by rape survivors to teach law enforcement officials – including police officers, detectives, prosecutors, etc. – how to improve their handling of rape cases would be beneficial. This type of training would allow the victims of sexual violence to describe their experiences and educate officers on how they should change their approaches to assist women in crisis following sexual assaults. In addition, it would provide an opportunity for *Han-Pu-Ri* to be practiced and the healing process to continue for both rape survivors and the larger community.

Despite these opportunities for change, it would be naive to claim that rape culture will cease to exist. However, we must confront it and make every effort to strive for social change. As Sharon Welch explains, we must have a mature attitude about our lived social reality. Nevertheless, instead of assuming that it is impossible to make change, we must move away from cynicism to a "joyful" resistance and focus on what can be done now that will help future generations.[9] Thus, it is imperative to stand in solidarity with women as they demand justice and confront the culture that has instigated their victimization.

Visions of healing

While the violated bodies and wounded spirits of women were the starting point of this study, the healed bodies and resurrected spirits of women are its objective. The testimonies of women from all parts of the world poignantly expressed their suffering, their grief, their *han*. This said, these stories also highlighted women as active agents in the transformation of the numerous injustices in their lives and their communities. Although rape will continue to exist and rape culture will continue to instigate sexual violence, women must voice their experiences of pain, suffering, and *han*. It is through this articulation that injustice will be heard, change can occur, and resurrection can begin.

This study began with my mother's story and the objective to speak her *han*; it is an act of *Han-Pu-Ri*. We must realize that only we have the power to interrupt our own suffering; only we have the ability to end our *han*. It is through courage and the refusal to give up on ourselves that we can find resurrection in the midst of such devastation. Our voice is key; silence only brings death. Our community is vital; isolation only fuels our demise. We must rage forward and reclaim our bodies, acknowledge our anger, and demand justice.

> In facing the ambivalent realities of our own lives and of the patriarchal societies in which we live, we are led to heal ourselves and each other. In the self acceptance and wholeness that come with healing, we are empowered to live by heart, to reach out to each other and to the whole aching and groaning cosmos in acts of honest remembrance and heartfelt connection.[10]

As we heal ourselves, we must stand as witnesses against all forces that seek to dominate, objectify, and dehumanize others. In doing so, we will travel together through this patriarchal terrain as active agents of liberation and it is here that we will continue to find momentary salvation.

Notes

1 Exum, "Feminist Criticism," p. 1.
2 See Trible.
3 See Nicholas Kristof and Sheryl WuDunn, *Half the Sky: Turning Oppression into Opportunity for Women Worldwide* (New York: Alfred Knopf, 2009), p. 155; Andrea Parrot and Nina Cummings, *Forsaken Females: The Global Brutalization of Females* (Oxford: Rowman and Littlefield, 2006), pp. 183–184.
4 See Michele Dillon, *Introduction to Sociological Theory* (Oxford: John Wiley and Sons, 2010); Anne Kingston, *The Meaning of Wife: A Provocative Look at Women and Marriage in the 21st Century* (New York: Farrar, Straus and Giroux, 2004).
5 Sandy Kobrin. "More Women Seek Vaginal Plastic Surgery." Women's ENews.org, November 14, 2004. Retrieved from: http://www.womensenews.org/story/health/041114/more-women-seek-vaginal-plastic-surgery.
6 Ruether, pp. 94–99.
7 Chung, *Struggle to Be the Sun Again*, p. 45.
8 Gebara, pp. 123–124.
9 See Sharon Welch, *A Feminist Ethic of Risk* (Minneapolis: Fortress Press, 2000).
10 Brock, p. 106.

Bibliography

Aalders, G.C. *Genesis*. Vol. 2. Grand Rapids: Zondervan, 1981.
Adams, Carol J. "'I Just Raped My Wife! What are You Going to do about it, Pastor?': The Church and Sexual Violence," in Emilie Buchwald, Pamela Fletcher, and Martha Roth (eds.) *Transforming a Rape Culture*. New York: Milkweed, 1993, pp. 57–86.
Adams, Carol J. and Marie M. Fortune (eds.). *Violence against Women and Children: A Christian Theological Sourcebook*. New York: Continuum, 1995.
Ahmed, Khalid. "The Sociology of Rape." *Slogan* February (1992): pp. 36–37.
Allen, Beverly. *Rape Warfare: The Hidden Genocide in Bosnia-Herzegovina and Croatia*. Minneapolis: University of Minnesota Press, 1996.
Anderson, A.A. *World Biblical Commentary: 2 Samuel*. Vol. 2. Dallas: World Books: 1989.
Askin, Kelly Dawn. *War Crimes against Women: Prosecution in International War Crimes Tribunals*. The Hague: Kluwer Law International, 1997.
Augustine. *The City of God*. Trans. Henry Bettenson, ed. David Knowles. Harmondsworth: Penguin, 1972.
Barstow, Anne (ed.). *War's Dirty Secret: Rape, Prostitution, and Other Crimes against Women*. Cleveland: Pilgrim Press, 2000.
Bart, Pauline and Eileen Geil Moran. *Violence against Women: The Bloody Footprints*. Thousand Oaks, CA: Sage Publications, 1993.
Bechtel, Lyn M. "What if Dinah is Not Raped? (Genesis 34)." *Journal for the Study of the Old Testament* 62 (1994): pp. 19–36.
Benedict, Helen. "The Language of Rape," in Emilie Buchwald, Pamela Fletcher, and Martha Roth (eds.) *Transforming a Rape Culture*. New York: Milkweed, 1993, pp. 101–106.
Beneke, Timothy. *Men on Rape: What They Have to Say about Sexual Violence*. New York: St. Martin's Press, 1982.
——"Jay: An 'Armchair' Rapist," in Patricia Searles and Ronald Berger (eds.) *Rape and Society: Readings on the Problem of Sexual Assault*. Oxford: Westview Press, 1995, pp. 55–57.
Bergen, Raquel Kennedy. *Wife Rape: Understanding the Response of Survivors and Service Providers*. Thousand Oaks, CA: Sage Publications, 1996.
Bernard of Clairvaux. *Selected Works*. New York: Paulist Press, 1987.
Bible and Culture Collective, The. *The Postmodern Bible*. New Haven: Yale University Press, 1995.
Bourke, Joanna. *Rape: Sex, Violence, History*. Berkeley: Shoemaker Hoard Publishing, 2007.

Bremmer, Jan. N. *The Apocryphal Acts of Paul and Thecla.* Leuven: Peeters, 1996.
——*The Apocryphal Acts of Peter: Magic, Miracles and Gnosticism.* Leuven: Peeters, 1998.
Brison, Susan J. "Surviving Sexual Violence," in Stanley G. French, Wanda Teays, and Laura M. Purdy (eds.) *Violence against Women: Philosophical Perspectives.* Ithaca: Cornell Press, 1998, pp. 11–26.
Brock, Rita Nakashima. *Journeys by Heart: A Christology of Erotic Power.* New York: Crossroad, 1988.
Brock, Rita Nakashima and Susan Brooks Thistlethwaite. *Casting Stones: Prostitution and Liberation in Asia and the United States.* Minneapolis: Fortress Press, 1996.
Brock, Rita Nakashima and Rebecca Ann Parker. *Proverbs of Ashes: Violence, Redemptive Suffering, and the Search for What Saves Us.* Boston: Beacon Press, 2001.
Brown, Brené. *Women and Shame.* Austin: 3C Press, 2004.
Brown, Delwin, Sheila Greeve Davaney, and Kathryn Tanner (eds.). *Converging on Culture: Theologians in Dialogue with Cultural Analysis and Criticism.* New York: Oxford University Press, 2001.
Brown, Joanne and Carole R. Bohn (eds.). *Christianity, Patriarchy, and Abuse: A Feminist Critique.* New York: Pilgrim Press, 1989.
Brownes, I. "Assailants' Sexual Dysfunction during Rape: Prevalence and Relationship." *Medicine, Science, and the Law* 31(4) (1991): pp. 322–328.
Brownmiller, Susan. *Against Our Will: Men, Women, and Rape.* New York: Simon & Schuster, 1975.
Buchwald, Emilie, Pamela Fletcher, and Martha Roth (eds.). *Transforming a Rape Culture.* Minneapolis: Milkweed, 1993.
Burgess, Ann Wolbert, A. Nicholas Groth, Lynda Lytle Holmstrom and Suzanne M. Sgroi. *Sexual Assault of Children and Adolescents.* Lanham: Lexington Books, 1978.
Bussert, Joy. *Battered Women: From a Theology of Suffering to an Ethic of Empowerment.* New York: Lutheran Church in America, 1986.
Calvin, J. *A Commentary on Genesis.* London: Banner of Truth, 1965.
Carmichael, Calum. *Women, Law, and the Genesis Traditions.* Edinburgh: Edinburgh University Press, 1979.
Carr, David. *Reading the Fractures of Genesis: Historical and Literary Approaches.* Louisville: Westminster John Knox Press, 1996.
Cassel, Eric. "Pain and Suffering," in Warren Thomas Reich (ed.) *Encyclopedia of Bioethics.* Vol. 4, rev. edn. New York: Macmillan Library Reference USA/Simon & Schuster Macmillan, 1995, pp. 2490–2496.
Chopp, Rebecca. "Theology and the Poetics of Testimony," in Delwin Brown, Sheila Greeve Davaney, and Kathryn Tanner (eds.) *Converging on Culture: Theologians in Dialogue with Cultural Analysis and Criticism.* New York: Oxford University Press, 2001, pp. 56–70.
Chung Hyun Kyung. "*Han-Pu-Ri*: Doing Theology from Korean Women's Perspective." *The Ecumenical Review* 40(1) (January 1988): pp. 27–36.
——*Struggle to Be the Sun Again: Introducing Asian Women's Theology.* New York: Maryknoll: Orbis books, 1990.
Clark, Ann. *Women's Silence, Men's Violence: Sexual Assault in England 1770–1845.* New York: Pandora, 1987.
Clement. "First Epistle of Clement to the Corinthians 6:2," in *The Apostolic Fathers.* Trans. Kirsopp Lake. LCL 24. Cambridge, MA: Harvard University Press, 1965.

Coats, George W. *Genesis with an Introduction to Narrative Literature*. Vol. 1. Grand Rapids: Eerdmans, 1983.
Cosgrove, Charles (ed.). *The Meanings We Choose: Hermeneutical Ethics, Indeterminacy, and the Conflict of Interpretation*. New York: T&T Clark International, 2004.
Cousins, Ewert. "Preface to the Series," in *World Spirituality: An Encyclopedic History of the Religious Quest*. Vol. 1. New York: Crossroad, 1987.
Criminal Code of the Russian Federation. "Crimes against Sexual Inviolability and Sexual Freedom of the Person. Article 131: Rape." Retrieved from: http://www.russian-criminal-code.com/PartII/SectionVII/Chapter18.html (accessed May 2013).
Daly, Mary. *The Church and the Second Sex*. Boston: Beacon Press, 1968.
———*Beyond God the Father*. Boston: Beacon Press, 1973.
———*Pure Lust: Elemental Feminist Philosophy*. Boston: Beacon Press, 1984.
———*Gyn/Ecology: The Metaethics of Radical Feminism*. Boston: Beacon Press, 1990.
Deacy, Susan and Karen Pierce (eds.). *Rapes in Antiquity*. London: Duckworth, 1997.
Department of Justice: Bureau of Justice Statistics. "Rape and Sexual Assault." 2009. Retrieved from: http://bjs.ojp.usdoj.gov/index.cfm?ty=tp&tid=317 (accessed May 2013).
Department of Justice: Federal Bureau of Investigation. "Appendix II: Offenses in Uniform Crime Reporting," in *Crime in the United States*. 2004. Retrieved from: http://www2.fbi.gov/ucr/cius_04/appendices/appendix_02.html (accessed May 2013).
Dillon, Michele. *Introduction to Sociological Theory*. Oxford: John Wiley and Sons, 2010.
Donaldson, Ian. *The Rapes of Lucretia: A Myth and its Transformation*. Oxford: Clarendon, 1982.
Dworkin, Andrea. *Pornography: Men Possessing Women*. New York: Plume, 1991.
———"I Want a Twenty-four Hour Truce during Which There is No Rape," in Emilie Buchwald, Pamela Fletcher, and Martha Roth (eds.) *Transforming a Rape Culture*. New York: Milkweed, 1993, pp. 11–22.
Engel, Mary Potter. "Evil, Sin, and Violation of the Vulnerable," in Susan Brooks Thistlethwaite and Mary Potter Engel (eds.) *Lift Every Voice: Constructing Christian Theologies from the Underside*. San Francisco: Harper & Row, 1990, pp. 159–172.
Equality Now. "Pakistan: The Hudood Ordinances – Denial of Justice for Rape: The Case of Dr. Shazia." *Women's Action* 26(1). Retrieved from: http://www.equalitynow.org/take_action/pakistan_action261 (accessed May 2013).
Estrich, Susan. *Real Rape: How the Legal System Victimizes Women Who Say No*. Cambridge, MA: Harvard University Press, 1987.
Evans, Lane. "News release." House Committee on Veterans' Affairs: Democratic Office. Retrieved from: http://veterans.house.gov/democratic/press/109th/9-29-05mst.htm (accessed July 2013).
Exum, Cheryl. *Fragmented Women: Feminist (Sub)versions of Biblical Narratives*. Journal for the Study of the Old Testament Supplement Series 163. Sheffield: Sheffield Academic Press, 1993.
———"Feminist Criticism: Whose Interests are Being Served?," in Gale A. Yee (ed.) *Judges and Method: New Approaches in Biblical Studies*. Minneapolis: Fortress Press, 1995, pp. 65–90.
Farley, Wendy. *Tragic Vision and Divine Compassion: A Contemporary Theodicy*. Louisville: Westminster John Knox Press, 1990.
———*The Wounding and Healing of Desire: Weaving Heaven and Earth*. Louisville: Westminster John Knox Press, 2005.

Fewell, Dana. *Reading Between Texts: Intertextuality and the Hebrew Bible.* Louisville: Westminster John Knox Press, 1992.

Flores, Theresa. *The Slave across the Street: The True Story of How an American Teen Survived the World of Human Trafficking.* Boise: Ampelon Publishing, 2010.

Fortune, Marie. *Sexual Violence: The Unmentionable Sin.* New York: Pilgrim Press, 1983.

Fortune, Marie and Cindy Enger. "Violence against Women and the Role of Religion." The National Online Resource Center on Violence against Women. http://www.vawnet.org/applied-research-papers/print-document.php?doc_id=411 (accessed October 2012).

Frederick, Sharon and the Aware Committee on Rape. *Rape: Weapon of Terror.* River Edge: Global Publishing Company, 2001.

Frymer-Kensky, Tikva. "Virginity in the Bible," in Victor Matthews, Bernard Levinson, and Tikva Frymer-Kensky (eds.) *Gender and Law in the Hebrew Bible and the Ancient Near East.* Sheffield: Sheffield Academic Press, 1998, pp. 79–96.

Gebara, Ivone. *Out of the Depths: Women's Experiences of Evil and Salvation.* Minneapolis: Fortress Press, 2002.

Gibbs, Nancy. "Sexual Assaults on Female Soldiers." *Time*, March 8, 2010.

Goodwin, Jan. "Sierra Leone is No Place to Be Young." *New York Times*, February 14, 1999.

Groth, Nicholas. "Motivational Intent in Sexual Assault of Children." *Criminal Justice and Behavior* 4(3) (1977): pp. 253–264.

Gunn, David. *The Story of King David: Genre and Interpretation.* Sheffield: Sheffield Academic Press, 1978.

Haeri, Shahla. "The Politics of Dishonor: Rape and Power in Pakistan," in Mahnaz Afkhami (ed.) *Faith and Freedom: Women's Human Rights in the Muslim World.* New York: Syracuse University Press, 1995, pp. 161–174.

"Harman Introduces Bipartisan Bill to Halt Rape and Sexual Assault in the Military." July 29, 2008. Retrieved from: http://harman.house.gov/2008/07/July29-MST.shtml (accessed September 2011).

Havrilla, Rebekah. "Hearing Testimony of Rebekah Havrilla Before the Military Personnel Subcommittee of the Senate Armed Services Committee." March 13, 2013. Retrieved from: http://www.armed-services.senate.gov/statemnt/2013/03%20March/Havrilla%2003-13-13.pdf (accessed May 2013).

Herman, Judith Lewis. *Trauma and Recovery.* New York: Basic Books, 1992.

Hope, A, and Eriksen, M. "From Military Sexual Trauma to 'Organization-Trauma': Practicing 'Poetics of Testimony'." *Culture & Organization* 15(1) (2009): pp. 109–127.

Human Rights Watch. *Crime or Custom: Violence against Women in Pakistan.* New York: Human Rights Watch, 1999.

Human Rights Watch Women's Rights Project. *The Human Rights Watch Global Report on Women's Human Rights.* New York: Human Rights Watch, 1995.

Hyun Young-Hak. "Minjung the Suffering Servant and Hope." Lecture given at James Memorial Chapel, Union Theological Seminary, New York, April 13, 1982.

Interpol. *Brazilian Penal Code: Article 213.* Retrieved from: http://www.interpol.int/public/Children/SexualAbuse/NationalLaws/csaBrazil.asp (accessed October 2010).

——*National Laws: Japan.* Retrieved from: http://www.interpol.int/Public/Children/SexualAbuse/NationalLaws/csajapan.asp (accessed October 2010).

Isherwood, Lisa (ed.). *The Good News of the Body: Sexual Theology and Feminism.* New York: New York University Press, 2000.

Isherwood, Lisa and Elizabeth Stuart. *Introducing Body Theology*. Sheffield: Sheffield Academic Press, 1998.

Jacobs, Susie, Ruth Jacobson, and Jennifer Marchbank. *States of Conflict: Gender, Violence and Resistance*. New York: Zed Books, 2000.

Jensen, Robert. "Cruel to Be Hard: Men and Pornography." Sexual Assault Report Spring (2004): pp. 54–58.

Jerome. "Epistle 22:5," in *Select Letters of St. Jerome*. Trans. E.A. Wright. LCL 262. Cambridge, MA: Harvard University Press, 1963.

Jung, Carl. Letters. ed. G. Adler. Princeton: Princeton University Press, 1973.

Kasinsky, Renee. "Rape: A Normal Act?" Canadian Forum September (1975): pp. 18–22.

Kasper, Walter. *The God of Jesus Christ*. New York: Crossroad, 1984.

Kersgaard, Scot. "Buck's Refusal to Prosecute 2005 Rape Case Reverberates in US Senate Race." *Colorado Independent*, October 11, 2010. Retrieved from: http://coloradoindependent.com/63491/bucks-refusal-to-prosecute-2005-rape-case-reverberates-in-u-s-senate-race (accessed June 2011).

Kimmel, Michael. "Clarence, William, Iron Mike, Tailhook, Senator Packwood, Spur Posse, Magic ... and Us," in Emilie Buchwald, Pamela Fletcher, and Martha Roth (eds.) *Transforming a Rape Culture*. New York: Milkweed, 1993, pp. 119–138.

Kingston, Anne. *The Meaning of Wife: A Provocative Look at Women and Marriage in the 21st Century*. New York: Farrar, Straus and Giroux, 2004.

Kobrin, Sandy. "More Women Seek Vaginal Plastic Surgery." Women's ENews.org, November 14, 2004. Retrieved from: http://www.womensenews.org/story/health/041114/more-women-seek-vaginal-plastic-surgery (accessed May 2012).

Koss, Mary and Cheryl Oros. "Sexual Experiences Survey: A Research Instrument Investigating Sexual Aggression and Victimization." *Journal of Consulting and Clinical Psychology* 50(3) (1982): pp. 455–457.

Kristof, Nicholas and Sheryl WuDunn. *Half the Sky: Turning Oppression into Opportunity for Women Worldwide*. New York: Alfred Knopf, 2009.

Lanzetta, Beverly. *Radical Wisdom: A Feminist Mystical Theology*. Minneapolis: Fortress Press, 2005.

Lee, Jae Hoon. *The Exploration of the Inner Wounds – Han*. Atlanta: Scholar Press, 1994.

Lee Oo Chung, "Korean Traditional Culture and Feminist Theology," in *The Task of Korean Feminist Theology*. Seoul: Korean Association of Women Theologians, 1983, pp. 74–86.

Lerner, Gerda. *The Creation of Patriarchy*. New York and Oxford: Oxford University Press, 1986.

Levenson, Jon. "I Samuel 25 as Literature and History." *Catholic Biblical Quarterly* 40 (1978): pp. 11–28.

Levenson, Jon and Baruch Halpern. "The Political Import of David's Marriages." *Journal of Biblical Literature* 99 (1980): pp. 507–519.

Levy, Barrie. *Women and Violence*. Berkeley: Seal Press, 2008.

Livy. *Ab Urbe Condita*. Oxford Classical Texts. Oxford: Oxford Press, 1974.

McConaghy, Nathaniel. *Sexual Behavior: Problems and Management*. New York: Plenum Press, 1993.

McInerney, Maud Burnett. *Eloquent Virgins: From Thecla to Joan of Arc*. New York: Palgrave Macmillan, 2003.

MacKinnon, Catherine. "Sexuality, Pornography, and Method: Pleasure Under Patriarchy." *Ethics* 99(2) (January, 1989): pp. 314–346.

——*Are Women Human: And Other International Dialogues*. Cambridge, MA: Harvard University Press, 2006.
Madigan, Lee and Nancy C. Gamble. *The Second Rape: Society's Continued Betrayal of the Victim*. New York: Lexington Books, 1989 [1991].
Mai, Mukhtar. *In the Name of Honor*. New York: Washington Square Press, 2006.
Malamuth, Neil. "Rape Proclivity Amongst Males." *Journal of Social Issues* 37(4) (1981): pp. 138–157.
Mananzan, Mary John, Mercey Amba Oduyoye and Elsa Tamez. *Women Resisting Violence: Spirituality for Life*. Maryknoll: Orbis, 1996.
Manlowe, Jennifer L. "Seduced by Faith: Sexual Traumas and Their Embodied Effects," in Carol J. Adams and Marie M. Fortune (eds.) *Violence against Women and Children: A Christian Theological Sourcebook*. New York: Continuum, 1995, pp. 328–338.
Miedzian, Myriam. "How Rape is Encouraged in American Boys," in Emilie Buchwald, Pamela Fletcher, and Martha Roth (eds.) *Transforming a Rape Culture*. New York: Milkweed, 1993, pp. 153–163.
Morris, David. *The Culture of Pain*. Berkeley: University of California Press, 1989.
MtJoy, Roxann. "The FBI's Shockingly Narrow Definition of Rape." September 15, 2010. Retrieved from http://womensrights.change.org/blog/view/the_fbis_shockingly_narrow_definition_of_rape (accessed October 2010).
Noddings, Nel. *Women and Evil*. Berkeley: University of California Press, 1989.
Odem, Mary and Jody Clay-Warner. *Confronting Rape and Sexual Assault*. Wilmington: Scholarly Resources, 2003.
Offence of Zina Ordinance (Enforcement of Hudood). 1979.
O'Sullivan, Chris. "Fraternities and Rape Culture," in Emilie Buchwald, Pamela Fletcher, and Martha Roth (eds.) *Transforming a Rape Culture*. New York: Milkweed, 1993, pp. 23–30.
Otwell, John. *And Sarah Laughed: The Status of Women in the Old Testament*. Philadelphia: Westminster Press, 1977.
Oxford English Dictionary. 2nd edn. Oxford: Oxford University Press, 1989.
Park, Andrew Sung. *The Wounded Heart of God: The Asian Concept of* Han *and the Christian Doctrine of Sin*. Nashville: Abingdon Press, 1993.
——*Racial Conflict and Healing: An Asian-American Theological Perspective*. Maryknoll: Orbis Books, 1996.
——*From Hurt to Healing: A Theology of the Wounded*. Nashville: Abingdon Press, 2004.
——"Sin," in Miguel A. De La Torre (ed.) *Handbook of US Theologies of Liberation*. St. Louis: Chalice Press, 2004, pp. 110–116.
Park, Andrew Sung and Susan L. Nelson (eds.). *The Other Side of Sin: Woundedness from the Perspective of the Sinned-Against*. New York: State University of New York Press, 2001.
Parrot, Andrea and Nina Cummings. *Forsaken Females: The Global Brutalization of Females*. Oxford: Rowman and Littlefield, 2006.
——*The Sexual Enslavement of Girls and Women Worldwide*. London: Praeger Publishers, 2008.
PBS. "Survivors Share Experiences of Sexual Assault in the Military." March 13, 2013. http://www.pbs.org/newshour/bb/military/jan-june13/sexualassualt_03-13.html (accessed May 2013).
Pedersen, Johannes. *Israel: Its Life and Culture*. 2 vols. London: Oxford University Press, 1959.

Pellauer, Mary. "A Theological Perspective on Sexual Assault," in Mary Pellauer, Barbara Chester, and Jane A. Boyajian (eds.) *Sexual Assault and Abuse: A Handbook for Clergy and Religious Professionals.* San Francisco: Harper & Row, 1987, pp. 82–91.

Pellauer, Mary, Barbara Chester, and Jane A. Boyajian (eds.). *Sexual Assault and Abuse: A Handbook for Clergy and Religious Professionals.* San Francisco: Harper & Row, 1987.

Penny, Laurie. "Steubenville: This is Rape Culture's Abu Ghraib Moment." *New Statesman*, March 19, 2013. Retrieved from: http://www.newstatesman.com/laurie-penny/2013/03/steubenville-rape-cultures-abu-ghraib-moment (accessed July 2014).

Peterson, Eugene H. *First and Second Samuel.* Louisville: Westminster John Knox Press, 1999.

Pierce-Baker, Charlotte. *Surviving the Silence: Black Women's Stories.* New York: W.W. Norton and Company, 1998.

Polaris Project. "Testimony of Anita." Retrieved from: http://actioncenter.polarisproject.org/the-frontlines/survivor-testimonies/38-testimonies/56-testimony-of-anita (accessed June 2011).

Pseudo-Lucian. *Lucius or The Ass, in Lucian.* Vol. 8. Trans. M.D. MacLeod. LCL 432. Cambridge, MA: Harvard University Press, 1969, pp. 52–145.

Quina, Kathryn and Nancy Carlson. *Rape, Incest, and Sexual Harassment: A Guide for Helping Survivors.* New York: Greenwood Press, 1989.

Raine, Nancy Venable. *After Silence: Rape and My Journey Back.* New York: Three Rivers Press, 1998.

Rankka, Kristine M. *Women and the Value of Suffering: An Aw(e)ful Rowing Toward God.* Collegeville: Liturgical Press, 1998.

"RapeLay." Wikia. Retrieved from http://gaming.wikia.com/wiki/Rapelay (accessed September 2010).

Reddington, Frances and Betsy Wright Kreisel. *Sexual Assault: The Victims, the Perpetrators, and the Criminal Justice System.* Durham, NC: Carolina Academic Press, 2005.

Reis, Pamela Tamarkin. "Cupidity and Stupidity: Women's Agency in the 'Rape' of Tamar." *Journal of the Ancient Near Eastern Society* 25 (1998): pp. 43–60.

Rivers, Carly. *Aphrodite at Mid-Century.* Garden City, NY: Doubleday, 1973.

Robinson, Gnana. *1 & 2 Samuel: Let Us Be Like the Nations.* Grand Rapids: Eerdmans, 1993.

Ross, Winston. "CNN Feels Sorry for Steubenville Rapists; World Can't Believe its Ears." The Daily Beast, March 18, 2013. Retrieved from http://www.thedailybeast.com/articles/2013/03/18/cnn-feels-sorry-for-steubenville-rapists-world-can-t-believe-its-ears.html (accessed March 2013).

Ruether, Rosemary Radford. *Sexism and God-Talk: Toward a Feminist Theology.* Boston: Beacon Press, 1983.

Ruff-O'Herne, Jan. *50 Years of Silence.* Sydney: Tom Thompson, 1994.

Rushing, Andrea Benton. "Surviving Rape: A Morning/Mourning Ritual," in Mary Odem and Jody Clay-Warner (eds.) *Confronting Rape and Sexual Assault.* Wilmington: Scholarly Resources, 2003, pp. 5–19.

Russell, Diana. *The Politics of Rape.* New York: Grune and Stratton, 1975.

Russell, Letty. "Authority and the Challenge of Feminist Interpretations," in Letty Russell (ed.) *Feminist Interpretation of the Bible.* Philadelphia: Westminster, 1985, pp. 137–146.

Russell, Letty (ed.). *Feminist Interpretation of the Bible*. Philadelphia: Westminster, 1985.
Sanday, Peggy Reeves. *The Socio-Cultural Context of Rape*. Washington, D.C.: United States Department of Commerce, 1979.
—— *Female Power and Male Dominance: The Origins of Sexual Inequality*. New York: Cambridge University Press, 1981.
—— *Fraternity Gang Rape: Sex, Brotherhood, and Privilege on Campus*. New York: New York University Press, 1990.
—— *Women at the Center: Life in a Modern Matriarchy*. New York: Cornell University Press, 2004.
Scarry, Elaine. *The Body in Pain: The Making and Unmaking of the World*. New York: Oxford University Press, 1985.
Schneider, Tammi J. *Judges*. Collegeville: The Liturgical Press, 2000.
Schneiders, Sandra M. "Spirituality in the Academy," in Bradley Hanson (ed.) *Modern Christian Spirituality: Methodological and Historical Essays*. Atlanta: Scholars Press, 1990, pp. 15–38.
Scholz, Susan. *Sacred Witness: Rape in the Hebrew Bible*. Minneapolis: Fortress Press, 2010.
Schroeder, Joy. *Dinah's Lament: The Biblical Legacy of Sexual Violence in Christian Interpretation*. Minneapolis: Fortress Press, 2007.
Schulenburg, Jane. *Forgetful of Their Sex*. Chicago: University of Chicago Press, 1983.
Schüssler Fiorenza, Elisabeth. "The Will to Choose or to Reject," in Letty Russell (ed.) *Feminist Interpretation of the Bible*. Philadelphia: Westminster, 1985, pp. 125–136.
Scully, Diana and Joseph Marolla. "'Riding the Bull at Gilley's': Convicted Rapists Describe the Rewards of Rape," in Patricia Searles and Ronald Berger (eds.) *Rape and Society: Readings on the Problem of Sexual Assault*. Oxford: Westview Press, 1995, pp. 58–73.
Seifert, Ruth. "War and Rape: A Preliminary Analysis," in Alexandra Stiglmayer (ed.) *Mass Rape: The War against Women in Bosnia-Herzegovina*. Lincoln: University of Nebraska Press, 1994, pp. 54–72.
Setrakian, Lara. "Saudi Rape Victim Tells Her Story: Victim to Receive Whipping and Jail for Being in Nonrelative's Car When Attacked." ABC News, November 21, 2007. Retrieved from: http://abcnews.go.com/International/story?id=3899920&page=1 (accessed June 2011).
Smart, Elizabeth. "Elizabeth Smart Speaks at Johns Hopkins University." May 6, 2013. Retrieved from: http://fox13now.com/2013/05/06/video-elizabeth-smart-speaks-at-johns-hopkins-university/ (accessed May 2013).
Sölle, Dorothee. *Suffering*. Philadelphia: Fortress Press, 1975.
—— *The Strength of the Weak: Toward a Christian Feminist Identity*. Philadelphia: Fortress Press, 1984.
Stiglmayer, Alexandra (ed.). *Mass Rape: The War against Women in Bosnia-Herzegovina*. Lincoln: University of Nebraska Press, 1994.
Stone, Ken. "Sexual Power and Political Prestige: The Case of the Disputed Concubines." *Bible Review* 10 (1994): pp. 28–31, 52–53.
Suetonius. *The Lives of the Caesars*. ed. J.C. Rolfe. New York: Macmillan, 1924.
Suh Nam-Dong. "Towards a Theology of *Han*," in The Commission on the Theological Concerns of the Christian Conference of Asia (ed.) *Minjung Theology*. Singapore: CCA, 1981, pp. 54–65.
Taesoo, Yim. *Minjung Theology: Towards a Second Reformation*. Singapore: CCA, 2006.

Tertullian. "Ad Martyras", in Alexander Roberts and James Donaldson (eds.) *The Writings of Tertullian*. Whitefish, MT: Kesslinger Publishing, 2011.

——*Apology*. CCSL 1:85–171. Turnout: Brepols, 1953.

Thistlethwaite, Susan Brooks. "'You May Enjoy the Spoil of Your Enemies': Rape as a Biblical Metaphor for War." *Semeia* 61 (1993): pp. 59–75.

Torjesen, Karen Jo. *When Women Were Priests: Women's Leadership in the Early Church and the Scandal of Their Subordination in the Rise of Christianity*. New York: HarperSanFrancisco, 1993.

Townes, Emilie (ed.). *A Troubling in My Soul: Womanist Perspectives on Evil and Suffering*. New York: Maryknoll, 1997.

Trible, Phyllis. *Texts of Terror: Literary-Feminist Readings of Biblical Narratives*. Philadelphia: Fortress Press, 1984.

Tsevat. Matitihu. "Marriage and Monarchical Legitimacy in Ugarit and Israel." *Journal of Semitic Studies* 3 (1958): pp. 237–243.

UNIFEM. *Women on the Frontline – Democratic Republic of Congo*. Canberra: Australian Development Cooperation, 2008.

Vachss, Alice. *Sex Crimes: Ten Years on the Front Lines Prosecuting Rapists and Confronting Their Collaborators*. New York: Random House, 1993.

Veselka, Vanessa. "The Collapsible Woman: Cultural Response to Rape and Sexual Abuse," in Lisa Jervis and Andi Zeisler (eds.) *Bitchfest*. New York: Farrar, Straus and Giroux, 2006, pp. 56–61.

von Rad, Gerhard. *The Problems of the Hexateuch*. New York: McGraw Hill, 1966.

Warshaw, Robin. *I Never Called it Rape: The Ms. Report on Recognizing, Fighting and Surviving Date and Acquaintance Rape*. New York: Harper & Row, 1988.

Welch, Sharon. *A Feminist Ethic of Risk*. Minneapolis: Fortress Press, 2000.

Wénin, André. *Studies in the Book of Genesis: Literature, Redaction and History*. Leuven: Leuven University Press, 2001.

West, Stuart. "The Rape of Dinah and the Conquest of Shechem." *Dor le Dor* 8(3) (Spring 1980): pp. 144–156.

West, Traci. *Wounds of the Spirit*. New York: New York University Press, 1999.

——*Disruptive Christian Ethics*. London: Westminster John Knox Press, 2006.

Wiesel, Elie. "The Holocaust as Literary Inspiration," in Elie Wiesel and Lucy Dawidowicz (eds.) *Dimensions of the Holocaust*. Evanston: Northwestern University Press, 1977.

Wiesel, Elie and Lucy Dawidowicz (eds.). *Dimensions of the Holocaust*. Evanston: Northwestern University Press, 1977.

Wimbush, Vincent L. "Biblical–Historical Study as Liberation: Toward an Afro-Christian Hermeneutic." *Journal of Religious Thought* 42(2) (Fall–Winter 1985–1986): pp. 9–21.

Winstead, Karen A. *Virgin Martyrs: Legends of Sainthood in Late Medieval England*. Ithaca: Cornell University Press, 1997.

Wisse, Ancrene. *Anchoritic Spirituality*. New York: Paulist Press, 1991.

Woolf, Virginia. "On Being Ill," in *The Moment and Other Essays*. New York: Harcourt Brace Jovanovich, 1948.

Wurthwein, Ernst. *The Text of the Old Testament*. London: SCM Press, 1980.

Young, Kathleen Zuanich. "The Imperishable Virginity of Saint Maria Goretti," in Carol J. Adams and Marie M. Fortune (eds.) *Violence against Women and Children: A Christian Theological Sourcebook*. New York: Continuum, 1995, pp. 279–286.

Index

Notes are referenced in the index with an 'n', for example xin2 would denote page xi note number 2.

Absalom 11–14, 27
Acts of Paul and Thecla 18–19, 90
adultery 16, 52, 63
ageism 67
Ahithophel 12
Amnon 11
Augustine 16–17

Beneke, Timothy 66, 70
Bible 5–9, 11, 111
"Blurred Lines" 75
Brock, Rita Nakashima 84, 101, 104–105, 109
Brownmiller, Susan 20, 25n91, 41, 63–64, 70, 73
Buck, Ken 76

Carl's Jr. ad 75
Catholic 19, 21, 48; *church* 20–21, 25n91, 36, 54, 90, 92
Central Park Jogger 72
Christianity 5, 17, 19, 21, 85, 101
Chopp, Rebecca 27
Chung Hyun Kyung 88, 101–103, 113
classism 67
Cousins, Ewert 84,
Culture 34, 55–58, 67–68, 83, 85, 94–97, 106–107; *dominant* 108; *of blaming* 69; *of silence* 106; *Western* 102; *see also* rape culture

Daly: 85
date rape; *see* rape
David (King) 7, 11–15, 27, 83, 102
Deuteronomy 13–14, 73
Dinah 7–9, 26, 73, 83, 90

Dolce and Gabbana 75
Dworkin, Andrea 66

evil 67–69, 85, 101; *moral* 67; *social* 67–69
Exum, Cheryl 6, 9–10, 15

Facebook 61, 74
feminism 61
Fortune, Marie 5, 8, 64

gang rape: *see* rape
Gebara, Ivone 105, 109, 113
gender 15, 62, 67, 70–71
General Hospital 74
Genesis 6–9
God 5, 12, 16–9, 21, 29, 32–33, 45–46, 52, 57, 83, 94, 96; *god as male* 85

Han x, xin2, 2, 4, 4n8, 83, 86–89, 91, 97, 101–109, 113–114
Han–Pu–Ri x, xin2, 2, 4, 100–109, 113–114
Hudood Ordinance 63
hymen 5, 16, 19, 111–112

Islam: *General Zia 63*; *Islamic law 63*; *Islamic society* 44
isolation 4, 69, 84, 91, 103, 104, 115
institutional violence 112
invisibility: 2, 4, 91–92, 101

Jerome 16–17, 89
Jesus 19, 85, 94; *Jesus Christ* 66
Judges 7, 9–10, 15, 26
Jung, Carl 88

Index

Kimmel, Michael 71
Korean Association of Women Theologians (KAWT) 102–103

language 71–72
law 14, 16, 31, 34, 38, 62–63, 78–79; *biblical* 14; *of Moses* 11,
law enforcement 78–80, 90, 112, 114
Levite 9
Lot's daughters 6
Lucretia 15–17, 26–27, 83, 89–90, 111
Luke and Laura 74

Masculinity 41, 70, 71, 76, 112
MacKinnon, Catherine 64–65
media 74–6
medical treatment 77–78
menstruation 84, 93
methodology 2–3
Moses 11
Ms. Potiphar 6
Mukhtar Mai 44–46, 65, 92–93, 96, 106–109, 113

National Crime Victimization Survey 62
Noddings, Nel 67–68
norms 11, 66–69

Park, Andrew Sung 2, 77, 80, 87–89, 93
patriarchy 68
patriarchal culture 61, 90, 103
Paul 18, 90
personal self 66, 86, 97;Pope Pius XII 20–21
pilegesh 7, 9–10, 12–15, 26; *David's pilegesh* 12–15, 26, 83; *unnamed pilegesh in Judges* 7, 9–10, 26
pornography 3, 19, 75
Potiphar's wife: *see Ms. Potiphar*
poverty 67
pressure cooker theory 3, 25n93, 64, 72
prostitution 57, 96, 102
Ptolemy 18
purity legends 3, 15–21, 83, 111–112

Qatif Girl 41, 43–4, 65, 92–93, 95–96

race: 4n6, 4n8, 37; *racism:* 67
rape: *acquaintance:* 34–38; *analysis of:* 61–80; *as torture:* 17, 19, 21, 45, 57, 66, 72, 105–106; *date – see acquaintance; defined:* 62–66; *function of:* 63–66; *gang:* 41–44; *honor:* 44–46; *in the media:* 74–76; *in religion:* 5–21; *in war:* 46–60; *marital:* 38–41; *military:* 50–55; *myths* 72–74; *second rape:* 76–77; *stranger:* 27–34; *testimony of:* 26–57; *texts:* 5–21; *sex trafficking:* 55–58; *see also sexual violence*
rape culture 1–4; *analysis of 61–80; as social evil* 67–70; *causing han* 2, 83–96; *confronting* 100–109; *defined* 1, 61–62, 66–67; *elements of* 70–79; *impact on victim* 26–57, 83–97; *in religion* 5–24; *rapist* 4, 8, 18, 26, 64–65, 70, 72–74, 76–77, 79, 88, 90, 92, 95, 106–108, 112; *testimony about* 26–58
RapeLay 75–76, 114
religion 1, 3, 4n8, 5, 21, 27, 34, 67, 90, 94, 111, 112
Ruether, Rosemary Radford 68–69, 85
Russell, Letty 6

Saint Agatha 19
Saint Agnes 19
Saint Apollonia 19
Saint Barbara 19
Saint Cecilia 19
Saint Katherine 19
Saint Lucy 19
Saint Margaret 19
Saint Margaret Mary Alacoque 85
Saint Maria Goretti 15, 20–21, 25n88, 26–27, 83, 89–90, 111
Saint Ursula 19
salvation 100–109, 113–115
Scarry, Elaine 91
Scholz, Susanne 8, 11
Schroeder, Joy 6, 11, 15, 17, 19
Seifert, Ruth 46, 64, 66
self–blame 2, 28, 83–91, 93–97
self–image 86, 100–101, 105, 108, 111–113
sexism 67
sexual assault: *see* rape; sexual violence
sexuality 3, 15, 20, 25n93, 37, 64, 66, 70–71, 93–94, 111–112
sexual violence 1–4; *analysis of* 61–80; *in a rape culture* 61–80; *in religion* 5–24; *healing* 83–97; *surviving* 83–97; *testimony of* 26–57; *see also* rape
shamanistic practice 4, 101
shame 9–11, 15–18, 21, 26, 28, 34, 44–46, 54, 57–58, 61, 64–66, 74, 76, 78–79, 83, 86, 88–97, 101, 105–106, 108, 111–113
Shechem 7–9
Slutwalk 104
Smart, Elizabeth 26
soul 2, 7, 18, 26, 84–85, 88
Speak Out 104

spiritual death 2, 4, 4n1, 4n8, 27, 83–97, 101, 109, 113; spiritual wounding 4n5, 26–28, 51, 65, 83, 88
spirituality 83–86
spiritual resurrection xin3, 2, 4, 27, 97, 100–110, 113
Steubenville 61, 75
suffering 1–4, 15, 17, 21, 27–28, 48, 50, 58, 67–69, 71–72, 80, 83–97, 101–102, 104–106, 108–109, 111–113, 114
survivor 4, 4n1, 15, 27, 54, 79, 114; *from victim to survivo:* 100–110

Take Back the Night 103–104
Tamar 7, 10–12, 26–27, 73, 83, 90
Thecla 18–19, 90, 111
theology 103, 109; *Christian* 83, 85, 100, 101
Tertullian 16–17, 89
testimony 2, 3, 4n5, 6, 26–58, 63, 73–74, 78, 83, 90, 91, 92, 95, 97, 103, 106
texts of terror 5, 111
Trible, Phyllis 5
Tryphaena 18
Twitter 61, 75

Uniform Crime Report 62
US Department of Justice 62

victim 19, 21, 23n47, 25, 26, 28, 31, 33, 37, 40–42, 51, 56, 61, 63–64, 66, 69–80, 98n15, 112–113; *blaming* 1, 3, 5, 7, 9–11, 16–18, 34, 38, 53, 65, 67, 69, 70, 72–74, 76, 79, 86, 89, 90, 96, 97, 111–112, 114; *experience of* 83–97; *to survivor* 100–110, 113; *victimization* 38, 54, 65, 69–80, 111
virginity 8, 15–21, 90, 94, 111–112
virginity repair 111
virgin martyrs 15, 19–21, 83

Warshaw, Robin 34
war 3, 10, 14, 24n58, 27, 41, 51, 67, 96; *rape within* 46–50; *weapon of* 14; *World War II* 1, 2, 4n3, 27
Welch, Sharon 114
Wiesel, Elie 27
women's experience 5, 17, 63, 103

Zina Ordinance 63

eBooks
from Taylor & Francis
Helping you to choose the right eBooks for your Library

Add to your library's digital collection today with Taylor & Francis eBooks. We have over 45,000 eBooks in the Humanities, Social Sciences, Behavioural Sciences, Built Environment and Law, from leading imprints, including Routledge, Focal Press and Psychology Press.

Choose from a range of subject packages or create your own!

Benefits for you
- Free MARC records
- COUNTER-compliant usage statistics
- Flexible purchase and pricing options
- 70% approx of our eBooks are now DRM-free.

Benefits for your user
- Off-site, anytime access via Athens or referring URL
- Print or copy pages or chapters
- Full content search
- Bookmark, highlight and annotate text
- Access to thousands of pages of quality research at the click of a button.

ORDER YOUR FREE INSTITUTIONAL TRIAL TODAY

Free Trials Available

We offer free trials to qualifying academic, corporate and government customers.

eCollections
Choose from 20 different subject eCollections, including:

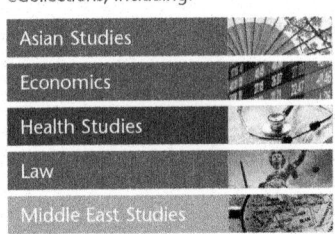

Asian Studies
Economics
Health Studies
Law
Middle East Studies

eFocus
We have 16 cutting-edge interdisciplinary collections, including:

Development Studies
The Environment
Islam
Korea
Urban Studies

For more information, pricing enquiries or to order a free trial, please contact your local sales team:

UK/Rest of World: **online.sales@tandf.co.uk**
USA/Canada/Latin America: **e-reference@taylorandfrancis.com**
East/Southeast Asia: **martin.jack@tandf.com.sg**
India: **journalsales@tandfindia.com**

www.tandfebooks.com

CPSIA information can be obtained
at www.ICGtesting.com
Printed in the USA
LVOW04*1525161116
513229LV00012B/117/P